Chase Mielke's profound and moving insights into the compassionate foundation of teaching will inspire those noble individuals we entrust with our children—teachers—to find passion and purpose. It is a must-read during these complex times.

—Dacher Keltner
Faculty Director, Greater Good Science Center, UC Berkeley
Author, *Born To be Good: The Science of a Powerful Life*
and *The Power Paradox: How We Gain and Lose Influence*

Mielke speaks to the reader with the heart of a teacher, the wisdom of an oracle, and the familiarity of a friend.

Readers will find research-based methodologies aimed at creating fundamental shifts in attitude, understanding, and behavior. A just-in-time antidote for the exhaustion afflicting our nation's teachers. An absolute must-read!

—Weston Kieschnick
Senior Fellow, International Center for Leadership in Education, Denver, CO
Best-selling author, *Bold School: Old School Wisdom + New School Technologies = Blended Learning That Works*

Chase Mielke does the work: he teaches in a classroom like yours and mine. He writes about resolving teacher burnout—and how you can, too, with strategies vetted by both research and real life.

Through it all, Chase offers us a coherent framework for understanding how to build flourishing lives inside and outside the classroom. This is a guide I've been looking for.

—Dave Stuart Jr.
Best-selling author, *These 6 Things: How to Focus Your Teaching on What Matters Most*

Chase Mielke is an exceptional educator and an exceptional human being, demonstrated by the authentic way he shares his personal story. His heartfelt writing will resonate with teachers as he shares with readers how to not "simply survive as an educator but thrive, personally and professionally."

—Bobbi DePorter
President, Quantum Learning Network / SuperCamp
Author of numerous books on teaching and learning and coauthor of *Excellence in Teaching and Learning: The Quantum Learning System*

THE
BURNOUT
CURE

THE
BURNOUT
CURE

Learning to Love Teaching Again

CHASE MIELKE

ASCD

Alexandria, Virginia USA

ASCD®

1703 N. Beauregard St. • Alexandria, VA 22311-1714 USA
Phone: 800-933-2723 or 703-578-9600 • Fax: 703-575-5400
Website: www.ascd.org • E-mail: member@ascd.org
Author guidelines: www.ascd.org/write

Ronn Nozoe, *Interim CEO and Executive Director;* Stefani Roth, *Publisher;* Genny Ostertag, *Director, Content Acquisitions;* Susan Hills, *Acquisitions Editor;* Julie Houtz, *Director, Book Editing & Production;* Darcie Russell, *Editor;* Judi Connelly, *Associate Art Director;* Donald Ely, *Senior Graphic Designer;* Valerie Younkin, *Production Designer;* Mike Kalyan, *Director, Production Services;* Trinay Blake, *E-Publishing Specialist;* Kelly Marshall, *Senior Production Specialist*

All web links in this book are correct as of the publication date below but may have become inactive or otherwise modified since that time. If you notice a deactivated or changed link, please e-mail books@ascd.org with the words "Link Update" in the subject line. In your message, please specify the web link, the book title, and the page number on which the link appears.

PAPERBACK ISBN: 978-1-4166-2725-8   ASCD product #119004   n3/19

PDF E-BOOK ISBN: 978-1-4166-2727-2; see Books in Print for other formats.

Quantity discounts are available: e-mail programteam@ascd.org or call 800-933-2723, ext. 5773, or 703-575-5773. For desk copies, go to www.ascd.org/deskcopy.

Library of Congress Cataloging-in-Publication Data
Names: Mielke, Chase, author.
Title: The burnout cure : learning to love teaching again / Chase Mielke.
Description: Alexandria, Va. : ASCD, [2019] | Includes bibliographical references and
    index.
Identifiers: LCCN 2018053341 (print) | LCCN 2018059241 (ebook) | ISBN
    9781416627272 (Pdf) | ISBN 9781416627258 (pbk.)
Subjects: LCSH: Teachers—Psychology. | Teachers—Attitudes. | Teaching—
    Psychological aspects. | Teacher turnover—Prevention.
Classification: LCC LB2840 (ebook) | LCC LB2840 .M45 2019 (print) | DDC
    371.102—dc23
LC record available at https://lccn.loc.gov/2018053341

28 27 26 25 24 23 22 21 20 19   2 3 4 5 6 7 8 9 10 11 12

To Bob

For giving me the permission and support to take risks

THE
BURNOUT CURE

Introduction

I'm sure you've seen multiple representations of teaching cycles, meticulously crafted with buzzwords: formative assessment; performance task; progress monitoring; data, data, data. But can we talk about the *real* teaching cycle? For many teachers, it looks like this:

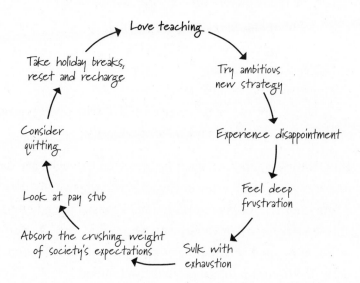

Your cycle of teaching might have additional phases, such as "Parent blame-storm," "Legislative letdown," and "Loss of respect and autonomy."

Though we experience different types of ups and downs, every educator experiences moments of doubt, defeat, and exhaustion. At a minimum, these moments distract us from our love of teaching. At most, they make us want to quit.

Have you been there? Questioning your decision to teach? Ready to turn away from this career that used to be a calling? If so, you're not alone. The statistics around teacher burnout and attrition aren't encouraging. Between 8 and 15 percent of teachers leave the profession every year (Ingersoll, Merrill, & Stuckey, 2014), and around 40 percent of new teachers will leave the profession within five years (Ingersoll, 2012).

Just a few years ago, I stood toe-to-toe with the quitting phase of teaching. Ten years into the career, I had had enough. I was brushing up my résumé, job searching each night, and looking into every alternative career route possible. You can probably guess some of the many factors that had burned me out:

- Challenging, disrespectful students
- Absurd pressures around testing
- Negotiation battles
- Stressed-out colleagues
- The dichotomy of uninvolved and overinvolved parents
- Adolescent cruelty and lack of integrity

Other factors weighed on me, too. I trudged through each day and came home to a colicky newborn and a wife who was fighting postpartum depression. My emotional bank was depleted, yet I sluggishly went back to work every day, wondering why I was doing it.

So, why am I writing a book about "thriving" when I was clearly declining not long ago? Because I rallied.

It was either coincidence or irony that, amid languishing personally and professionally, I was teaching a positive psychology class that I had developed on human flourishing. The class is an elective open to all students at the high school where I teach, but it's designed to target students who are languishing in their lives—asking the same questions, at the teenage level, about the "why" of adversity and the "how" of happiness that we ask as adults.

I'm convinced that if I hadn't known about the research related to positive psychology—if I hadn't practiced what I taught to my students—I would have bitterly walked away from my calling and left the field of education. Instead, I engaged every mindset, every cognitive shift, every research-based practice I knew and lifted myself back to loving my job.

Although counteracting the desire to quit required the deepest commitment, this was not the first time I had to rally against the temptation. I have faced burnout, exhaustion, and the urge to give it all up multiple times. No doubt you have too. But I have no doubt that you also know, somewhere deep in your mind, that education is worth the effort and the struggle.

This book is a response to a critical question: *How do we refuel, reenergize, and reframe to be our best as teachers so we can give our best to learners?* I've spent over a decade studying and teaching positive psychology, which essentially poses—and answers—this question more broadly: *What research-based practices help people and communities flourish?* My purpose in writing this book is to share what I've learned to help you rally when you feel burned out, to not simply survive as an educator but to thrive, personally and professionally.

The practices in this book are more than just research-based ideas. They are my lifelines when I have a rough day, my lenses for realizing why teaching is my calling. Each practice has been through the "real life and rigorous research" test. In other words, it is supported by a multitude of peer-reviewed research studies and it helped me (and countless others) improve well-being in real life, particularly regarding teaching and coaching. Every chapter will help you understand the gist of the concept and then outline some specific strategies, practices, and resources I've used personally and taught to thousands of students and educators.

But I can't simply throw a bunch of random concepts at you. We need a framework, a model, a—dare I say it—cycle to help us improve our well-being more methodically.

The Empowered Thriving Model

Just as there are countless representations of the cycles of teaching, there are countless models for learning. The model I'm offering, which I call the "Empowered Thriving Model," is one of those implicit models that is a part of almost everything we do, whether it is teaching a student about energy convergence, helping a colleague with a pedagogical strategy, or trying to shed those holiday calories.

After years of studying the research on human well-being, I realized that we can approach thriving like we approach teaching: by beginning with the end in mind. Regardless of what outcome we seek, the process for change usually looks like this:

Awareness → Attitude → Action → Outcome

If we were dealing with physical well-being, our *outcome* might be "Lose five pounds of excess weight." To reach that outcome, we would need to change some *actions*, such as by replacing soda (or adult beverages) with water. Or we might add a serving of fruits or vegetables to every meal. Actions affect outcomes.

We also know that before we change our actions, we often need to shift our *attitude*. Our attitude is how we frame and feel about a concept or action. For example, if our attitude is that all types of calories are the same, it might be harder to resist that extra donut in the staff lounge. If instead we shift our attitude to think about different calories as different qualities of fuel—that we are placing diesel, unleaded, or premium into our system with each food choice—we might be more likely to skip the donut as a subpar fuel. Attitude influences action.

Before the attitude shifts, however, we need to develop *awareness*. We need to know and see certain things that we didn't see previously. For example, if we become more aware of the difference in how simple carbs from corn syrup affect our energy compared with complex carbs from whole grains, that awareness can sway our attitude.

This ability of awareness to shift attitude is why we teach students explicit concepts. For example, once they are aware that states of matter are a result of molecular density and particle movement, they can reframe their attitude toward state changes like water coming to a boil or ice freezing on a bridge.

The model I teach for influencing thriving emerged from seeing this process of *Awareness → Attitude → Action → Outcome* everywhere in education. But rather than *only* starting with awareness, we can instead consider it more like this:

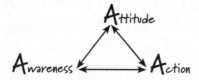

Shifting from a process to a cycle (as represented by the triangle) creates two key changes: upward spirals and different access points.

Adjusting one element—action, attitude, or awareness—creates an upward spiral that affects the others. Throughout this book are examples that show how changing an attitude can shift both our awareness and our actions, and how a change in action, like sending someone a letter of gratitude, might make us more aware of things that enhance our well-being. Changing one element influences all three.

We also now have different access points rather than one first step. The chapters in this book are grouped according to whether a concept will help shift an awareness, an attitude, or an action. You can therefore skip to any chapter that sounds interesting. If you want to add some specific actions to your week that will make you happier, jump to those chapters marked "Action." If you recognize that you seem to be aware of only what's wrong with the world, begin with some "Awareness" chapters. Note that the practices described in one chapter can be used to enhance the practices covered in another chapter.

Critical Questions

Before diving in, we should address some critical questions and consider some caveats for getting the most out of this book (and life).

Critical Question #1: Can People Actually Influence Their Well-being?

Genetics or choices? Wiring or upbringing? It's the nature-versus-nurture conundrum. We often debate the extent to which aspects of our life—personality, well-being, genius—are genetically preset. Thankfully, social science has shown that nature and nurture are like two giant roots making up the base of the same tree.

Although many of the personality traits we possess are genetic, we have a lot of control over our psychological thriving (or languishing). Researchers Kennon Sheldon and Sonja Lyubomirsky perused hundreds of studies on the factors influencing well-being (2007). Their resulting Sustainable Happiness Model states that the variances of our well-being are split into three parts. (See figure on the next page.)

Genetics can influence our emotional range; however, our genetics are neither our destiny nor our doom when it comes to well-being. We can still make a huge difference in the level of our happiness through our daily actions, especially if we use intentional, research-based practices.

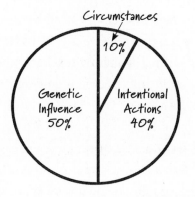

That 40 percent slice of the pie is what we're aiming to shift in this book. Sure, having control over 40 percent isn't as great as having control over 97 percent. But if you're willing to drive extra distance to save a few cents per gallon on gasoline, you're probably willing to boost your well-being by shifting a few mental perspectives and actions.

Also consider that you *already* are trying to influence your well-being every day. You have hobbies, you interact with (or avoid) other people, you make decisions—all of which influence your happiness. This book is designed to help you sift through actions that have been linked to well-being and add other research-based options to your tool kit.

Critical Question #2: Isn't This "Fix Yourself" Approach Ignoring the Need to Fix the System?

One of the biggest misconceptions of improving well-being is that by focusing on internal issues, we're ignoring or becoming complacent about external issues. I wholeheartedly agree that countless problems within the educational system are leading to teacher burnout and dissatisfaction; these aren't solved by ignoring them or putting the onus on teachers to simply "be happy and deal with it."

To expend the energy necessary to address large-scale issues, however, educators need to *have* energy in the first place. Education can't improve with languishing teachers who don't have the energy to pour passion into problem solving. We *give* our best when we *are at* our best.

At the same time, I'm also a realist. We cannot always rely on or control the large-scale, systemic changes that can reduce teacher burnout. But we can rely on and control ourselves in the meantime. Investing in our own well-being is not the ending point—it's a starting point.

So, for those of you who fight the good fight daily, consider this book a shot of cognitive caffeine to help you keep fighting for yourself, for your students, and for society.

Critical Question #3: Isn't This "I Want to Be Happy" Stuff Pretty Selfish?

Another misconception about well-being is that the pursuit of happiness is a selfish endeavor. We might picture a self-centered hedonist who takes and consumes without any care for others. But this idea of "me, me, me" is only one—often fruitless—approach to well-being.

The world of positive psychology distinguishes between *hedonia* and *eudaimonia*. Put simply, hedonia is "feeling good," whereas eudaimonia is "feeling purposeful." Both can be important contributors to well-being, but my experiences (and a lot of studies) have shown that eudaimonia can have a more transformative and long-term effect on happiness.

One underlying thread of "purpose" is doing things that benefit others. It's possible to experience hedonia without involving anyone else, but it's hard to feel purposeful without helping others. And, as we'll see in many examples in this book, finding more purpose can also make us feel good in the moment. In pursuing more eudaimonia, then, we can increase our well-being while helping people and improving the world around us.

But you already know this because your career in education is rooted in eudaimonia. So increasing your well-being is not a selfish endeavor. It's a critical part of your professional development that also happens to benefit your personal development.

Critical Question #4: Do I Have to Be Happy All the Time?

Being affected by adversity is a part of life—no matter what our age, demographic, or circumstance. But our culture can also make people feel guilty about not having that perfect, social-media-worthy life.

As a high school teacher, I often find myself coaching teenagers in crisis to repeat and understand this mantra: *Don't feel bad about feeling bad.* Like teenagers, we often feel pressure to look, feel, and act happy all the time, so we find ourselves in a downward spiral. *I'm stressed. But I shouldn't be stressed because so-and-so doesn't seem stressed. Am I malfunctioning? I should be happy. Be happy. Go! Why isn't this working?*

We can think of emotion the same way we think about teaching. We know not every lesson is going to be perfect, but we still pursue excellence. We know not every day is going to be great, but we still pursue happiness. So we don't have to be perfect to make progress. To keep my students from sulking, we complete the mantra like this: *Don't feel bad about feeling bad. But don't give up on believing in the potential for good.*

If you're having a crappy day, own it! Be real and reflect on that discontent. And then rally. Rally with new awareness, new attitudes, and new actions to give yourself hope.

Caveats

With some questions addressed, here are some caveats to consider.

Caveat #1: "Positive Thinking" Isn't Always Enough

We have a lot of work to do as a society when it comes to understanding mental health. Our culture seems to have adopted an approach to well-being that is expressed as "If you're sad, snap out of it." Well-being is a complex thing, influenced by more than just thoughts. We have unique blends of genetic factors, brain chemistry, circumstances, and hormones that each affect our happiness in their own way. This book is focused on just a slice of those many factors: metacognition and actions to improve well-being.

However, I will never endorse a belief that "thinking differently" is enough for every challenge for every person. The models and strategies outlined in this book are not a panacea; nor are they a replacement for support from a licensed doctor or therapist. If you have felt depressed or anxious for some time, save this book for another day and contact someone who can give you the one-on-one care that you deserve.

Caveat #2: There Is No Magic Wand

One of my pet peeves is someone trying to present a single well-being concept as a "secret to happiness." The sales pitch suggests that just knowing a "thing" will be all we need to live a happy life. Improving our well-being is not easy work. In fact, we can expect that any change to our perception of how happy or sad we are won't last long.

Researchers refer to this reality as *hedonic adaptation*—our tendency to return to set points after emotional changes. Studies of lottery winners, cancer survivors, and paraplegics have revealed a tendency for human well-being to adapt (Diener, Lucas, & Scollon, 2009). A lot of factors influence our adaptation, but generally, humans return to our set points.

On one level, this return is a good thing. If we have an adversity (an emotional trough), we know that it is possible and probable that we won't always feel terrible. The downside is that this is also true of the boosts (the emotional peaks). For example, we might feel joy when we finally are able to buy that slightly nicer used car on our teacher salary. Eventually, though, the thrill wears off and we get used to what we have.

And there are key differences between our adaptation to good events compared to bad events. We tend to return to a baseline more quickly and consistently after positive events. On the flip side, when we have a bad event our adaptation back to our set point often takes longer, and, with some major adversities, such as losing a job, we might not fully get there (Diener et al., 2009).

This doesn't mean we should give up on our well-being. Instead we should do the opposite: be more active in taking care of ourselves. Just as eating one salad isn't enough to take care of our physical well-being, doing one action and expecting a massive change in our level of happiness won't work. We can't live at the peak of positive waves forever, especially knowing that life will hit us with troughs. Instead, we can try to ride the waves as long as we can, emerge from the troughs as quickly as we can, and through the process, raise the sea level of our well-being over time.

You've invested a lot of time and money into your career as an educator. You've spent years giving effort and attention to helping your students and your community. But all of that giving comes at a cost to your well-being. When you're constantly burning, you risk losing your flame. Whether you're at your last flicker or simply know that your light can burn brighter, it's a good time to invest in your own well-being.

I hope that the awarenesses, the shifts in attitude, and the actions described in this book can reignite your passion as they have fueled mine. We give our best when we are at our best. Here's to taking the time to be your best.

1

Awareness:
Becoming a Goodness Curator

*The greatest weapon against stress is our ability
to choose one thought over another.*

—William James

Surprockets (n): the surprise items left in your pocket at the end of a day of teaching. Examples include broken pencils, dry erase markers, rubber bands, fidget spinners, stickers, glitter, paper clips, trendy tiny toys, sticky notes with reminders you forgot to follow up on.

My wife once pulled a human tooth from her pocket. For a split-second, I thought she was about to murder me after revealing her second life as a serial killer. Then I remembered that a child's tooth is not an uncommon thing for a 2nd grade teacher to have in her pocket. Thankfully it was in a plastic bag and she knew which kid had lost it.

We spend our days as educators collecting things from our classrooms and students, but we also spend our days collecting experiences, observations, and memories. While the tangible things weigh down our pockets, the intangible collections can either weigh down our minds and hearts or enlighten us with a sense of accomplishment and hope.

A question that is critical to our well-being is this: What observations and memories do we spend our days collecting?

Each day we make decisions about what experiences we carry with us. Sometimes we bring home the good things— stories of student resilience, recognition of our self-worth, affirmation that what we do matters. But more often it seems we collect the heavy things— memories of student misbehavior, rumination about things beyond our control, fixation on failures.

If we collect too much of the negative and carry it too often, our work can feel heavy and hopeless. At the end of the day, the burdens we carry may leave us with a discontent that disrupts our mind as we try to sleep and taints our morning as we wake up.

The way we frame our awareness each day can have a profound impact on our well-being, engagement, and sense of purpose. I say this from experience. I've had moments—days, weeks, entire school years—when I collected the negatives to the point of almost giving up this job I love. In those times, however, it was helpful to know about the human brain—how awareness patterns can be built and broken, how memory is fallible, and most of all, how the reality I was seeing as a teacher was just a tainted *version* of reality.

Understanding how the brain works can help us understand how to collect more positive experiences, which makes us more resilient teachers without losing the high standards and critical-thinking skills that make us effective in our jobs. In this chapter we'll look at the impact of becoming "goodness curators," sifting through the many versions of reality to collect the memories and experiences that help us thrive personally and professionally. Goodness curation involves two simple steps: choosing to focus on the good things and savoring these good things more frequently and deeply.

Why Memory Collection Matters

Here's a happiness question: Did you have a good day? Take a moment to think about your answer. Then go deeper. On what did you base your answer? Chances are, your answer hinged upon two things: your current mood and whether you recalled pleasant or unpleasant memories.

Consider the relationship between mood and memory as analogous to a thriving (or languishing) garden. Our mood is the quality of the soil and the weather. We can make choices that influence our mood, like going for a walk (Miller & Krizan, 2016) or listening to some good music (Schäfer, Sedlmeier, Städtler, & Huron, 2013). But to some extent, mood shifts are beyond our control. Mood will fluctuate based on things like our hormones and our circadian rhythms.

In gardening, we can prepare for the weather and adjust to it, but we can't control it. Our memories, though, are like the seeds and our actions are like watering the garden. We actually *do* have a lot of influence over our memories. We can decide what things we focus our attention on. We can influence how they replay in our minds (and how often we replay them). In other words, we can choose to plant good seeds and to put our energy into tending them.

The seeds we collect and tend matter because to a large extent we base our life satisfaction on our memories. The *intensity* of the positive memory or emotion isn't the deciding factor. Two factors are more important: *frequency* and *recency*.

Frequency Matters More Than Intensity

Although we remember significant events, many social psychologists argue that our subjective well-being is based more on how often we have positive experiences than on how intense they are (Diener, Sandvik, & Pavot, 2009). Thankfully, then, we don't have to have the most euphoric day of teaching to say we're in a good place. Instead, having a handful of good experiences might matter more.

Recency Matters More Than History

Before you take out that tally sheet and start counting memories, consider that recency matters more than history. Studies have found that we base our subjective well-being on the most recent three months of memories (Suh, Diener, & Fujita, 1996). Additionally, the most recent memories we recall can skew our view of our well-being (Kahneman, 2010). In psychology this phenomenon is known as the "peak-end rule." I call this the "final-class effect." If my last class or lesson of the day goes well, I leave my classroom thinking, "Today was solid." If, however, I end my day with classroom chaos, I go home sulking and feeling terrible—regardless of whether every other class period or lesson went well. Recency and resolution matter for our satisfaction.

Memories: The Ghosts of Past, Present, and Future

We can also understand the relationship between memory curation and well-being through our thoughts of the past, the present, and the future. Obviously, our past is our collection of memories. But what we recently focused on or experienced can also affect our present thoughts and awareness. For example, consider the "bad-lesson-hangover effect": if we bomb a lesson, even if it ended in the past, we may still be ruminating about it in the present. Past experiences can inform our present emotional state, even if the connection is only implicit (Hersher, 2017).

Additionally, when we consider our future possibilities, we touch up our past memories, basing our optimism or pessimism to some extent on our memory bank (Seligman & Tierney, 2017). If we find out our boss is going to observe us tomorrow, our expectations hinge upon the memories we've curated. If we've built memories that see observation as a source of helpful feedback, we look forward to tomorrow. If we've built memories of feeling criticized, we dread it.

Chapter 2 includes more strategies for influencing our awareness of the present, and Chapter 5 offers a more in-depth look at optimism or pessimism regarding our future. For now, realize that the memories you curate—the narrative of your past—also affect your present and future well-being.

So, how often do we, in our role as educators, find ourselves curating the bad—concentrating only on what's wrong with our students, our schools, our society? Before you groan at the thought that what follows is going to be another one of those false-optimism, "pretend life is always glowing" sort of approaches, take a deep breath. Shifting our focus to positives doesn't mean ignoring the negatives entirely. A good gardener doesn't ignore weeds, but he also doesn't spend the whole day pulling them at the expense of watering and tending the good seeds. We don't have to ignore the fact that education has unpleasant aspects, but we don't have to carry the ugliness with us.

Principles of Awareness

It's possible to curate more positive experiences, especially if we know some key principles of how our awareness shapes our well-being.

Principle #1: Subjective Reality—
Our Reality Is What We Make It

One of the first things that struck me when I started studying positive psychology was the focus on "subjective" well-being
rather than "objective" well-being. I wondered why the emphasis
wasn't more on the objective. For physical health, we use objective
measures such as blood pressure and cholesterol levels. Surely we
could simplify the study of happiness and use objective measures
such as wealth and physical health metrics.

It didn't take me long to see that both research and life experience show that well-being really is more subjective than objective (Diener, 2000). Take a classroom example: the B+ grade.
Objectively, one could argue that a B+ is a solid grade, showing a
high level of skill or conceptual knowledge. But, as every teacher
knows, a B+ will create elation and hope in one student, and anxiety and despair in another.

Put simply, our sense of well-being has more to do with how
we *feel* about our objective reality than the reality itself (a theme
we'll explore in more depth in Chapter 3). Business school professor Srikumar Rao (2010) describes this in terms of "mental
models"—the way we frame or label our experiences in the world.
For example, if someone cuts us off in traffic, we really don't know
why he did so. Maybe he's a jerk, or maybe he's rushing to the hospital because he got a call that his wife is in labor. We don't know,
but we use a quick, subjective mental model to make sense of the
objective reality. Or say a student falls asleep in class. Do we think,
"She fell asleep because she doesn't take school seriously and
doesn't respect me," or do we think, "Maybe she had a rough night
at home and is sleep deprived"? Is that e-mail from a parent really
accusatory, or are we adding our own interpretation of the tone
and intention?

The objective reality is most often neutral, but our subjective
response to it is what influences our well-being. The good news is

that we can choose what mental model we employ in response to an objective reality. The bad news is that our brain is often biased toward the negative.

Principle #2: Negativity Bias— *Bad Is Stronger Than Good*

Motivation can be summed up in two words: *avoid* or *approach*. Human brains have thousands of years of evolution rooted in the following two choices: approach the treat, avoid the threat. Between those two choices, however, our brain prioritizes "avoid the threat." We are wired to search for and assume dangers. Why? Because if we don't "approach the treat" (the fruit high in the tree), we still might have other opportunities in the future. But if we don't "avoid the threat" (the snake in the grass), this day could be our last.

Thus, the brain has evolved toward a negativity bias. The amygdala, which processes emotions (namely, fear), is one of the most connected parts of the brain; it has routes to almost every other function. It also butts right up to the hippocampus, which converts short-term memory into long-term memories. We're wired to better remember unpleasant experiences (Manns & Bass, 2016) and are conditioned to search for, remember, and prioritize threats more than treats. Couple that negativity bias with a job in education, which is often about identifying deficits and improving existing conditions, and it's easy to see why staying positive in this career can be difficult.

However, the fact that the brain has priorities doesn't mean we should just accept the bias. As a parallel, our bodies have also evolved to crave fats and sweets in order to have fuel reserves in the event we have to run from some wild beast. But that doesn't mean, thousands of years later, we should turn the bulk candy bins into our daily buffet.

Having a negativity bias is no reason to give up on looking for positives. It is, instead, the reason why we need to more proactively look for positives. And, because the brain is malleable, we can—with effort—dampen the negativity bias.

Principle #3: Neural Firing—*Neurons That Fire Together, Wire Together*

If you have kids of your own, you remember the challenge of choosing names for a child when you're an educator. You have so many associations with specific names that those feelings become automatic. The naming conversation between me and my wife sounded like this:

"What about 'Miles'?"

"Nope. I had a Miles who was grumpy and weird. What if we name him 'Jack'?"

"Oh lord, no. Don't you remember the Jack I had two years ago who ate his own boogers!? I don't want a booger-eater name. Maybe 'James'?"

"Ehhh. What if he's skinny? Kids will call him 'Slim Jim' his whole life. I've heard kids do that."

The associations we make between names and feelings don't come out of nowhere. They exist because we've created neural connections in our brain between a specific name and a set of memories or feelings. Every psych-nerd knows the simplified version of "Hebb's postulate," introduced by Canadian psychologist Donald Hebb in 1949: "Neurons that fire together, wire together." In other words, every time we do something, think something, or experience something, our neurons leave little "tracks," or imprints. Do something often enough and these tracks become paths, which can become roads and then highways.

Thankfully, these neural tracks are not permanent. The brain is plastic, constantly changing the number and strength of neural connections. For example, there is a set of motor neurons that fire when you lift your left thumb. A different set fires when you move your left index finger. What happens if tragedy strikes and that left index finger gets chopped off? Do those motor neurons for the lost finger just hang out in isolated sadness? Nope. It turns out that they too, in a sense, get "chopped." When certain neurons are no longer used, that "real estate" gets invaded by surrounding properties—a process called *cortical reorganization*. Lose an index finger and the neural space grows for your thumb and middle finger (Doidge, 2017). Use it or lose it; the brain is always changing.

On one level, the concept of "neurons that fire together, wire together" explains why we can get stuck in ruts of negativity. The more we are aware of the negatives and the more we talk about them, the more we fire neurons associating those memories with an unpleasant emotion. If we do this often enough, we build a negativity superhighway in our brain. Now those negative memories are easier to recall, and they connect more quickly to new experiences.

Conversely, this principle gives us hope for rewiring ourselves to form more "positive highways." If we choose to focus our awareness on positives in our world, we can forge new paths. This choice—to rewire positive associations with our days, our jobs, our relationships—has a powerful double effect: focusing on the good not only helps us see more good, it also helps us ignore petty irritations.

Principle #4: Inattentional Blindness— *We See Only Part of the Picture*

Imagine you're walking one day along a route you follow often. Part of a normal day, right? Not quite. A short distance away, a clown is riding a unicycle. You'd notice that, right? Maybe. But maybe not—especially if you were talking on your cell phone.

Researchers from Western Washington University found this phenomenon to be true (Hyman, Boss, Wise, McKenzie, &

Caggiano, 2010). When people were focusing on a cell phone conversation, 75 percent of them didn't remember seeing a unicycling clown.

This study is one of many demonstrations of an effect known as "inattentional blindness." If you want to experience it, stop reading right now and search the phrase "awareness test" on YouTube.

The awareness test is a re-creation of one of the "invisible gorilla" studies that measured inattentional blindness. In another classic study, researchers gave 24 radiologists pictures of lung scans. The radiologists were tasked with identifying abnormalities in lung nodules. Although the radiologists did a great job finding the abnormalities, they did a terrible job noticing an image of a gorilla that had been digitally inserted into the picture. Even though eye scans showed that they looked at the gorilla image as they searched, 83 percent of the radiologists didn't recall actually seeing it (Drew, Võ, & Wolfe, 2013).

The gist is this: because the brain has selective attention, when we focus our awareness on one set of stimuli, we notice it more, but we often *don't* notice other stimuli. Focus on your phone call and you'll conduct a conversation but not notice the clown. Focus on enforcing one classroom rule, like no chewing gum, and you'll see all the chompers going to town but not notice as many kids texting on their phones below their desks. Cast as a rule of behavior, this principle can be expressed in this way: *When I look for X, I notice less Y.*

We can't underestimate the importance of this rule in a discussion of well-being. It plays out in many ways. Consider these:

- When I pay attention to the bad, I don't notice the good.
- When I complain about what I don't have, I'm not grateful for what I do have.
- When I focus on the problems of tomorrow's adults, I don't notice their potential.

- When I look for what my third-period students will do wrong, I miss what they do right.

The choice of what we attend to—what enters our awareness—has a compounding effect on our well-being.

Principle #5: Memory Reconsolidation —*Memories Change*

Just as every psych-nerd knows the phrase "neurons that fire together, wire together," most brain junkies also know the initials *H. M.* The subject of perhaps the best-known case study in cognitive psychology, Henry Molaison suffered brain trauma when he was a kid: a bike slammed into him, torqueing his body and causing severe damage to the limbic system of his brain. After years of seizures, Henry consulted neurosurgeon William Beecher Scoville, who specialized in lobectomies. In 1953, Scoville snipped and removed the damaged parts of Henry's brain, including his hippocampus. Success! No more seizures. But also failure. From that point forward, Henry lost the ability to form new memories ever again (Dittrich, 2017).

Henry's tragedy helped us understand the role of the hippocampus in forming memories. But decades of study revealed something else: Henry lost his old memories faster than average. Before the surgery, his hippocampus hadn't just formed new memories; it had also fine-tuned old ones.

The new understanding is this: every time we recall a memory, our hippocampus helps reconsolidate it. One byproduct of this process is that our memories change each time we recall them (Bridge & Paller, 2012). In fact, our mood or mental priming at the time of recall can influence this shift. For example, imagine you watch a dinner-date scene from a movie and then have to recall details. If you were hungry when you watched it, you might have stronger recall about the food that was ordered. If you had heartbreak on your mind, you might have zeroed in on the couple's tense, awkward moments.

We can again see how this process influences our positive memory bank: if we shift our awareness to some of the good things in our life and then recall those positives, we may strengthen them, curating more "permanent pieces" in our collection.

Let's wrap all of these concepts together into an example. Imagine you have a new student coming from another district. Some of your colleagues say they heard this new kid is a behavioral nightmare. This shot of negative gossip taints your reality before the student even steps into your classroom (subjective reality). The first day he enters your room, you're on edge, paranoid, and concerned, looking for signs of trouble (negativity bias). Sure enough, he appears to scowl and delays getting started on the first assignment you give him, sitting closed off and silent. You associate this behavior with the last challenging kid you had, thinking, "Oh, great; another one of those types" (neural firing). All day, you seem to notice every minor issue—he texts on his phone or gets distracted; he talks to other kids instead of reading; he doesn't even make eye contact with you.

The "problem child" narrative in your head builds all day, to the point you don't notice some other details. For example, he did raise his hand to ask where the bathroom is. He picked up and handed back a classmate's pencil when she dropped it. He actually said good-bye to you when he left the room. All of these incidents faded into the background behind the negatives (inattentional blindness).

In the staff lounge and at home, you vent about your worries, the imperfect behaviors, the fears—staining your memories (memory reconsolidation) a deeper shade of negative (neural firing). Without an intentional shift in awareness, you've spent an entire day curating negative after negative, not considering the other realities—that this kid is going through a major life transition that might not be pleasant, that he might be just as paranoid and pro-tective as you are, that there were a number of positive behaviors.

If we're going to thrive as educators, and not just survive, we have to intentionally and proactively confront our mental mod-els and our cognition and develop patterns of positive awareness. We have to become "goodness curators." We need to collect just as many moments of triumph and memories of affirmation. What's the best way to begin this process? Give it a day—as described in the next section.

Noticing the Good

The first week of my positive psychology class, I give students their hardest assignment of the trimester:

> Go 24 hours without voicing a complaint, criticism, or gripe. If you catch yourself complaining, start the clock over. See how long it takes you to get a 24-hour stretch without negative speech.

There's no grade or evaluation for the assignment, of course. It's a "life assignment." And there are caveats:

- You can't just build up all your negatives, wait 24 hours, and then spew them out in a fit of rage.
- Addressing true injustices is fair game, as long as you're actually addressing the issue and not just griping.
- Complaint baiting is not allowed. Don't bring up a topic that you know someone else will complain about just so you can nod in agreement.

The next day we check in. Usually only a couple of students admit they were successful. Others either forgot to do the task or kept slipping. We then have some engaging conversations. We note how we forget to avoid complaining, suggesting that we need to *remind* ourselves to not complain for even just one day. We discuss "contextual complain spaces," areas in which we are more prone to gripe than others. We share about how much we notice others' negativity when we make "not complaining" an awareness.

Having a perfect day is not the end goal. Instead, we're trying to establish an awareness about how we view and approach the world. The 24-hour "no-complaining challenge" reveals how we tend to focus on the bad and ignore the good.

The challenge is also about breaking and making patterns. We're trying to break our pattern of curating the bad things in our day and make a new pattern for noticing and reminiscing about the good.

Twenty-four hours, of course, aren't going to permanently shift our patterns. As I tell my students, a healthful diet doesn't consist of one day spent undoing years of bad habits. Similarly, one day of focusing on positives can't rewire years of negativity bias and awareness habits. But every great change—whether in our personal lives or historically—begins with one day of action.

Becoming a goodness curator can be the jolt we need to make teaching worthwhile again. It can transform how we interact with our students and staff, even our family and friends. And we have nothing to lose by trying it. We'll continue to live our reality regardless of whether we try to make it more positive or not. But we'll still have to choose what reality we see. So, if you're ready to begin choosing a more empowering, fulfilling, and worthwhile reality, let the curation begin.

Life Assignments

The following "assignments" are some of my favorite ways to build a collection of good things.

Assignment #1: Take On the No-Complaining Challenge

I recommend everyone try the no-complaining challenge. This challenge is like a life audit: you'll step back and see how your mind works. There are a couple of routes you can take:

- **Option A:** Don't tell anyone you're doing the challenge. Simply give it your all and notice if people seem to shift in their interactions with you, especially people who know you well, like your partner, friends, or family.
- **Option B:** Enlist others. Get a partner or a handful of colleagues (or students) together who want to take on the challenge. Having others join you in the challenge enables you to keep each other accountable and provides a debriefing group for talking about the experience.

Remember that the idea isn't to find perfection; it's to make progress in identifying and reducing negativity bias.

Assignment #2: Add a "Peak-End Ritual" to Your Day

One of the greatest lessons I've learned about parenthood is that rituals matter. Parenting books and gurus talk about having bedtime rituals to help kids go to sleep. But the gurus are missing a huge question about such rituals: What's in it for me? I might sound pretty selfish, as providing a good night's sleep for my child should be the end goal. But every parent knows how much work it takes to build and maintain that ritual.

Fortunately, I've learned that the ritual is worth it not only for my son's sleep, but also for my well-being. As mentioned earlier, due to the "peak-end rule," recency and resolution matter for our memory and satisfaction. So, if I have a "bedtime-means-war" experience putting my toddler down to sleep at night, I'm likely to say I had a rough day. But if he goes the "snuggle-and-be-sweet" route, I'll feel like my day was amazing. And my thoughts at the end of the night matter because soon I'll be sleeping (or ruminating) and consolidating my version of reality into my memories.

My wife and I have habituated positive rituals into our child's bedtime routine. For example, even if my son has had a day of mega-tantrums, I make sure that I sing to him and kiss him goodnight—even when I'm grouchy. These rituals are positive ends to an otherwise challenging day. They give me a piece of goodness to collect to show me that the whole day wasn't bad.

Consider building a peak-end ritual into your school day. Before leaving your class, you could do one of the following:

- Ask yourself, what was your "win of the day"?
- Play a mood-lifting song as you do a final organization of your room or desk.
- Have a "victory session" rather than a "vent session" with colleagues.
- Write down a specific goal for tomorrow. Reflect on the progress you made today with the goal you set yesterday.
- Send a quick e-mail message to a parent, sharing something positive about one of your students.
- Write a positive affirmation on your board that students will see when they walk in the next day.

Also try some peak-end rituals at home in the evening. Check out some of the other practices described in this book, such as mindfulness meditations (see Chapter 2) or gratitude journaling (see Chapter 3).

Assignment #3: Start a Jar of Goodness

Get a large jar. Each day, recall one positive memory, write it on a slip of paper, and place it in the jar. At the end of the year (or sooner, if needed), pull out the slips of paper and reflect on the many positive memories you have.

Assignment #4: Reminisce About Your Reason for Becoming a Teacher

My students often ask me why I became a teacher. Based on their reactions to my response, they seem to expect me to say, "Because I was inspired by so-and-so" or, "I had this class that changed me." Neither of these was my reason, though. Truthfully, I was a defiant, antagonistic little punk. As an upperclassman, I skipped school often; I pulled pranks; I got kicked out of Spanish class permanently.

Despite my discontent with school, I remember the exact moment I decided to become a teacher. I was about to skip school again, most likely aggravated by some teacher and thinking, "I can't wait to get away from this place and never come back." Then, like getting smashed between the eyes with clarity, I had another thought: "That's one of the most selfish ideas ever—running from a problem rather than fixing it." That moment I decided that I wanted to be the teacher I didn't have in high school.

My aversion to school was a product of not having positive relationships with my teachers. In hindsight, of course, I can see that I had some great teachers. My issues with teachers were my version of reality as a teenager (I hadn't yet realized the importance of goodness curation). Nevertheless, my inspiration to teach was the desire to deliver what I had lacked. I wanted to build positive relationships with challenging students to help them find a better path—and for them not to simply infer that someone cared about their well-being, but to know it every day.

When we're frustrated as teachers, we often ask ourselves, "Why do I continue to do this?" But a more powerful question is "What inspired me to do this in the first place?" I've questioned my decision to stay in education many times. Every time I do, though, I bring myself to that moment in high school—having an epiphany that I could do something good for others.

Take some time and reminisce about your reason for teaching. Even though it has probably shifted since you started and the memory has been reconsolidated many times, recall the spark that led you to do this work. Write it down, talk about it, mull it over on your drive to school, post about it online—do whatever it takes to recall the empowering reasons you got into this career. That memory shouldn't be stuffed in the back of the museum; it should be the centerpiece.

Assignment #5: Celebrate with Others

Just as art curators don't have to be the ones who make the art, goodness curators don't have to be the source of positive things to take note of. Instead, we can celebrate the good with others. One way of doing this is "active constructive responding."

Say a student shares some good news about playing well in her soccer game over the weekend. Imagine how you might respond. Here are some possibilities:

- Point out the negatives of the event (active destructive): "Hmm. You should be careful; I just read about the long-term effect of concussions from soccer."
- Ignore or brush off the good news (passive destructive): *Nod head, continue to organize desk.*
- Give a vague and clichéd response (passive constructive): "That's pretty neat."
- Share authentic support and curiosity (active constructive): "That's awesome to hear! Tell me more about it."

A group of studies found that when people seek out others and discuss good things, it boosts their positive emotion and well-being to a point beyond the benefits of the good event itself. Additionally, if their partner gives an active-constructive response, it boosts the positive effect even more (Gable, Reis, Impett, & Asher, 2004). Celebrating others improves our relationship, allows us to share some goodness, and helps ignite the sharer's positive emotion.

This outcome doesn't mean we need to stop what we're doing and dive in every time a kid shares some good news. We all know how time consuming that would be, especially with elementary students who love to share that cool thing their cousin's friend's mother did 17 months ago. But consider offering some active-constructive responses in situations like these:

- With your partner or other key relationships in your life
- With a student you'd like to have a more positive relationship with
- When you're having a rough day and could use a boost of something good
- Tomorrow

Assignment #6: Curate "Emodiversity"

Many people think that happiness simply means pleasure in the moment (*hedonia*, as discussed in the Introduction). We become disappointed, then, when we don't experience pleasure all the time or the feeling doesn't last long. Being a goodness curator means recognizing the many different positive emotions and experiences that make up our well-being. For example, here's a list of some of the most common positive emotions felt by people everywhere:

- Serenity: sense of calm and contentment
- Interest: deep curiosity about a topic or an experience
- Hope: sense that the future will be positive
- Pride: satisfaction with the work or effort one produced
- Inspiration: motivation to take positive action
- Joy: boost of positive feeling, often associated with a surprise
- Awe: feeling overwhelmed with greatness of something on a large scale
- Amusement: experiencing genuine laughter
- Gratitude: recognition of the good things in one's life

Some of these emotions are context dependent, whereas others we can choose to experience. For example, awe is usually triggered by something grand in nature (I can't simply walk into the chaotic hallways of a high school and force myself to be in awe). Gratitude, on the other hand, can be sparked intentionally (a concept that we'll explore in Chapter 3).

Variety, beyond being the "spice of life," can be good for our health. One study looked at the positive and negative "emodiversity" of 175 adults and found that individuals who had a range of different positive emotions had lower inflammation in their bodies, regardless of whether their emotion was more or less positive or negative compared to others (Ong, Benson, Zautra, & Ram, 2018).

When collecting good things in your world, look for the range of different kinds of positives. Before leaving work each day, review the list of common positive emotions and consider at least one you experienced. But don't obsess over finding a range of positive emotions. If you spend too much time trying to figure out whether something is or isn't inducing happiness, the effort might be counterproductive. A good art curator doesn't spend every second analyzing whether every object is art or not—she simply notices it when it's there.

Developing the awareness needed to become a goodness curator isn't easy. I recall, during the year I almost quit teaching, deciding to focus on the good the moment I stepped into the school. Within the first 30 seconds of entering the building, I heard a student scream perversely and profanely across the hallway at another kid. It was like a kick to the shins of my positivity plan.

I had to make a choice. Actually, I had to make a couple. Choice one was the decision to address the issue of the screaming profanity, which I did (true issues should not be ignored). But then I had a more powerful choice: to let that moment dictate my day, framing every interaction I had around what's wrong with the world, or to still look for and curate the good in my school, my students, and my choice to teach. It wasn't hard to find positives—it just required a different lens.

Awareness: Being Mindful

You can't stop the waves, but you can learn to surf.

—Jon Kabat-Zinn

How much time should I give them to finish this reading? My room smells funky... teenage hormones probably. Should I cold-call on my students when they finish reading? No, a pair-share first. Am I doing too many pair-shares? Is that kid texting? No, just scratching his leg. I wonder if they have that taco bar in the cafeteria today. For real, what's that smell. Is it me? Did I put on deodorant? Some of them are finished reading. What was that mind-blowing question I was going to ask them... shoot. I had it a minute ago. I wonder if my son ate another rock at day care today. I hope not. How many small rocks can a small child eat safely? I need to buy some air freshener for this room.

Welcome to the chaotic mind of an educator. Whether it's prepping our next words, pondering what happened during the last lesson, or anticipating our next meeting, we often live everywhere but in the present moment. And if we *are* focused on what we're doing, we're often tense, evaluating every decision and observation.

What if our habits of frantic thinking and circular fretting are wreaking havoc on our well-being? What if our greatest hurdle to our present happiness is that we aren't *aware* of what's happening in the present?

In this chapter we explore the two-headed beast of the unmanaged mind: rambling and ruminating. We'll not only understand how rambling and ruminating affect our well-being, but also learn how to tame the two heads of the beast.

Rambling

How often do human minds wander? Ten percent of the time? Thirty-three percent of the time? How often has your mind already wandered since starting this chapter?

Researchers have provided some good answers to this question, collecting a lot of data to better understand what we think about and how a wandering mind affects our well-being. Matt Killingsworth (2013) and a crew of researchers collected 650,000 real-time reports from 15,000 people of all ages around the world. Randomly, an alert would go off asking participants to respond to three questions:

1. How do you feel?
2. What are you doing?
3. Are you thinking about something other than what you're doing? (And if "yes," is it a pleasant, neutral, or unpleasant thought?)

So, how often *do* human minds wander? The answer: we spend 47 percent of our waking hours thinking of something other than what we're doing. We are not present for *half* of our waking hours.

Mind-wandering can have benefits. Some aspects of mind-wandering help us come up with creative solutions or achieve aha moments. However, Killingsworth's data reveal that, more often than not, people are *less* happy when their minds are wandering. And the data show a causational effect. It isn't that we are unhappy and so we drift to pleasant dreams. Instead, mind-wandering tends to *precede* unhappiness (Killingsworth, 2013).

So, what's happening when we let our mind wander? And why is doing so reducing our sense of well-being? For those answers, we need to see what happens when the brain is in default mode.

No matter what time of day or type of thought, our brain is "in motion" as different parts are processing—an ecosystem never at rest. When we're actively focused on something (e.g., absorbed in an enjoyable, challenging hobby), a "task-positive" network of the brain is active (Hasenkamp, Wilson-Mendenhall, Duncan, & Barsalou, 2012). I refer to this as a Focused Attention Network. However, when we aren't focused on the external task at hand, our brain activates a network known as the Default Mode Network.

The Default Mode Network can challenge our well-being for a variety of reasons, including the following:

- When our thoughts are rambling, we aren't in a "flow state," a deep and often satisfying engagement in a challenging and interesting task (Csikszentmihalyi, 2009).
- When we focus on the past and the future, we aren't savoring the present moment and cultivating positive emotions.
- When we divide our attention, we make more mistakes and often take longer to complete important tasks (Medina, 2014).

But there's more. Not only does this mind-rambling Default Mode Network run opposite of savoring and flow, it also sets the stage for negative rumination. This is an important point: When our brain engages the Default Mode Network, it creates ideal conditions for the second head of the beast—rumination, which can be the true source of unhappiness.

Let's say your mind is like a classroom. Imagine you've provided students with an interesting and challenging learning task. They are engaged in the task. They are present. They are in the zone and experiencing flow. Although the occasional student might cause a distraction, he's easy to manage. Now imagine that you give students free time to do whatever they want. They soon run amok. Distractions and misbehaviors pop up. This is the Default Mode Network at work. A mind without focused attention often finds mental mischief and leaves the gate open for the beast of rumination to devour our well-being. Rambling leads to ruminating.

Ruminating Our Own Ruin

It's the middle of the night and you *know* you need to sleep. Your brain starts rambling through random thoughts, but soon you can't stop rehashing a scene or problem. Maybe you're thinking of perfect comebacks to that student's snarky question, or you have a school board presentation in a few days that you haven't started preparing for. Now you're stuck in a rumination loop.

In its most basic form, rumination is the experience of a repetitive thought. The word *ruminant* comes from the Latin *ruminare*, meaning "to chew over again." Just as ruminant animals rechew food to help digestion, rumination is theorized to have evolved in humans as a helpful mental process: pondering problems can help us generate solutions.

But, like many processes that serve a purpose in human evolution, rumination sometimes kicks in when it doesn't need to, like when a song plays in your mind over and over again. Much of our rumination, though, isn't about catchy pop songs. More often we ruminate about problems, real or imagined, from our past or from our simulated future.

You may be thinking, isn't focusing on a problem the *opposite* of mind-wandering? If we were actually addressing the problem, then we would have focused attention. However, we typically *aren't* dealing with problems that are the subjects of our ruminations. We're postulating, then trying to get our minds off the stress, only to see it "wander" back into our thoughts. Rumination is the fly buzzing around a television screen. It flies away but circles back to smack itself against the screen and disrupt our focus.

Although we may *think* this rumination is helping us solve problems by planning ahead, research finds that negative rumination makes us *worse* at problem solving (Lyubomirsky & Nolen-Hoeksema, 1995). Most of the time, we're simply spinning negative thoughts and emotions on a loop, rather than planning.

Our ramblings and ruminations are like an emotional acceleration system. Our rambling Default Mode Network opens up the throttle for worry and stress to go full blast. What we need, then, is a logical brake system. We need the ability to dampen our spiraling and cycling thoughts. That braking system is our Focused Attention Network. And, to give it a tune-up, we need to practice mindful awareness.

Mindfulness

What's the opposite of mind-wandering? Focused attention.

What's the opposite of obsessing about the past or the future? Being aware of the present.

What's the opposite of worry and evaluation? Detaching our judgment.

Introducing the counteraction to rambling and rumination, that thing you keep hearing and reading about: mindfulness.

Mindfulness is currently a hot topic of research. Although there's a lot about it that we don't know yet, what we do know offers much promise. For example, a meta-analysis of 39 research studies found moderate to strong effect sizes for mindfulness interventions on well-being. For the average person, mindfulness practices led to reduced anxiety (0.63 effect size) and increased positive mood (0.59). For those with high levels of anxiety, the effects were stronger (0.97 anxiety reduction; 0.95 positive mood increase (Davies, 2011).

Aside from decreasing anxiety and boosting our mood, benefits of mindfulness have included stronger interpersonal relationships (Barnes, Brown, Krusemark, Campbell, & Rogge, 2007), better sleep (Carlson & Garland, 2005), better focus and attention (McGreevey, 2011), and increased body satisfaction (Albertson, Neff, & Dill-Shackleford, 2014), to name a few.

Most important for the classroom, there's growing evidence that mindfulness affects teacher stress management *and* the culture of the class (Roeser et al., 2013). One study randomly assigned 224 urban elementary teachers to either a mindfulness-based stress management program or a control group (Jennings et al., 2017). The teachers were then tracked and observed while teaching. Those who experienced mindfulness training improved their emotional regulation and reduced their psychological distress and urgency about time. Classroom observations showed that these teachers also had more positive interactions with students—taking more calming deep breaths, remaining curious instead of rushing to judgment and punishment when students misbehaved, and even smiling more.

I was slow to accept the value of mindfulness. In my studies, I had seen it come up often in religious and spiritual history. But as a pragmatic person, I didn't understand what mindfulness had to do with me. Although the psychological basis of mindfulness piqued my curiosity, it wasn't until I started practicing it—even for a few minutes a day—that I realized the pervasive benefits of having a more mindful awareness.

Before we get into the basics of mindfulness practice, let's see how your thoughts work. Here's the simple task:

1. Set a timer to go off in one or two minutes.
2. Once you start the timer, try to maintain your attention solely on your breathing.
3. Focus on each inhale, visualizing the air entering and filling your lungs. Then, focus on the exhale slowly leaving your nostrils.

4. Close your eyes and continue to focus on your breathing. Each time you catch your mind drifting to a thought *other* than your breathing, simply return your focus back to your inhales and exhales.

How'd it go? If you're like me, you probably felt wildly incompetent at this task, thoughts drifting repeatedly. This simple "pretest" tells us how overpowering our Default Mode Network can be (and how weak our Focused Attention Network is).

If you struggled to maintain focus, you might think, "This isn't for me because I can't do it." Actually, the opposite is true. The harder it is to maintain focused attention, the more we may *need* to practice mindfulness. If you said, "I can't jog 20 yards without getting winded," it would be odd to then think, "I'm out of shape; cardio must not be for me." The worse shape we're in, the more important it is that we work out.

There are many ways to increase mindfulness, some of which I will outline later. Despite these variations, all of these practices hinge upon two basic concepts:

- Purposefully trying to maintain focus on experiences in the present moment (focusing on the present)
- Trying to refrain from evaluating or judging (accepting the experience)

Focusing on the Present

As educators, our world is plagued with events that divide our focus and shift thoughts from the present. Technology beeps and flashes, hitching us to hundreds of distractions in and beyond the classroom. Although we may have moments when we are present with our experience, typically our awareness shifts quickly.

We may see our rambling thoughts as a nuisance to our attempts to focus. However, if we reframe mind-wandering, we can leverage it to improve our Focused Attention Network.

View drifting thoughts as resistance training for focus. Each time your thoughts drift from the present, you have an opportunity to shift back and strengthen your focus. Just as resistance training changes muscular strength and efficiency, mindfulness practice changes the brain (Hölzel et al., 2011). Don't get frustrated, then, at the challenge of returning your focus. Welcome the opportunity for an attention-workout repetition.

In its most basic form, this is one of the main practices of mindfulness meditation. Although the *goal* is to maintain a focus on the present, the *practice* involves starting over whenever we notice that our minds have wandered. Some say that mindfulness meditation is the "art of beginning again."

Once we shift our awareness to the present moment, we transition into shifting our emotional connection with the present, accepting and experiencing the moment as it is rather than ruminating about it. It's important to note that mindfulness is not just about paying more attention; it's about paying *different* attention. We move from our default *evaluating* mode to a more calming and grounding *experiencing* mode.

Accepting the Experience

We are a motivated species. (Even that student avoiding class work is motivated. Look at his level of dedication to repeatedly deconstructing and reconstructing his pen.) Our drive to "do" things makes it challenging to fully experience life as it is.

In their book *The Mindful Way Through Depression*, a group of mindfulness gurus, including Mark Williams of the Oxford Mindfulness Center and Jon Kabat-Zinn of the University of Massachusetts Medical School, discuss how mindfulness differs from our usual "do stuff" mode—and why it's critical for increasing our well-being (Williams, Teasdale, Segal, & Kabat-Zinn, 2007).

They divide awareness into two types: our *doing* mode and our *being* mode. Our doing mode is the type of thinking we use to analyze and solve problems. As noted earlier, problem solving can be a good thing, but the authors discuss how it often leads to rumination and overthinking. In doing mode, everything we do is through the lens of comparison—how it *could* or *should* be rather than how it *is*. Sounds like a typical day in the classroom, right?

The being mode, according to Williams and his colleagues, is different:

> In being mode, we discover we can suspend evaluating how our experience "should" be or "ought" to be, of whether it is "correct" or "incorrect," of whether it is "good enough" or "not good enough," or of whether we are "succeeding" or "failing," even whether we are "feeling good" or "feeling bad." Each present moment can be embraced as it is, in its full depth, width, and richness, without a "hidden agenda" constantly judging how far our world falls short of our ideas of how we need it to be. (p. 65)

If you're picturing someone "experiencing the present" as a floating, unmotivated sloth, adjust that image. The authors stress, "We can still act with intention and direction" (p. 65). In fact, we're more *intentional* in our actions when we're mindful. Rather than stress-induced ruminations tainting our decisions, we act more objectively.

For example, imagine a student had an emotional meltdown yesterday. You may still be ruminating about it today. Today, that student starts to ask you some questions. If you're in normal *doing* mode, you may feel your emotions rise as you think, "Here we go again. Another meltdown in progress." Your focus narrows on all the things this kid does to annoy you. Judgment is now tainted with a host of emotions, many of which are overly reactive.

What if you could dampen the emotional overload for a moment and *observe* the student? What if you remained open to what the student needed—listening fully—and calmly helped him de-escalate his worry rather than escalating your own stress? Both the student *and you* would benefit from this moment of objective, rational thinking. Take it from mindfulness maestro Thich Nhat Hanh:

> During the moment one is consulting, resolving, and dealing with whatever arises, a calm heart and self-control are necessary if one is to obtain good results.... If we are not in control of ourselves but instead let our impatience or anger interfere, then our work is no longer of any value. (1975, p. 14)

Mindfulness is not being devoid of emotion. Instead, it is experiencing the present in full awareness. Consider these possibilities:

- Imagine being stuck behind that slow-moving first-year student and disengaging your stress, seeing instead an opportunity to look around and smile at students.
- Imagine eating lunch and savoring each bite, rather than mindlessly scarfing it down.
- Imagine seeing the uniqueness of the student in front of you, rather than having your mind ramble and rage about all the other things you *could* be doing.

Mindfulness is a full engagement in life. It is finding the richness in how life *is* instead of only seeing deficits in how life *could* or *should* be.

If it sounds like I'm getting fired up by this stuff, it's because I am. When I reached the end of my fuse with the most challenging, disrespectful class I ever taught, mindful breathing helped me stay rational and objective. When I came home after an exhausting day of teaching, mindful awareness helped me keep a calm head, be patient with my colicky newborn son (and distraught wife), and still find joy in being a dad. Mindful awareness has brought more meaning, more gratitude, and more calm to my life as a teacher, a father, and a spouse than any other cognitive change.

Life Assignments

Mindfulness is an antidote to the ruminating, rambling habits that plague our well-being as teachers. Although the world of mindfulness is expansive, here are a few assignments incorporating research-based practices that have helped me develop a more mindful awareness and a less ruminating and rambling mind.

Assignment #1: Use Mindfulness Triggers

You're probably already thinking, "When do I have time to meditate? I barely have time to eat lunch." We'll set aside the probability that we waste time doing mindless things. If you're looking for a brief boost of mindful awareness, use a *mindfulness trigger*.

First, identify a common event or situation in which you go into either rambling mode or negative rumination mode. Here are some examples:

- Rambling Triggers
  - Cleaning rituals (washing hands, cleaning dishes)
  - Sipping your morning beverage
  - Students walking into your classroom in the morning
  - Driving (e.g., pulling into a parking lot)

- Ruminating Triggers
  - Being stopped at a red light
  - Being stuck behind slow-moving students in the hallway
  - Having to wait in line
  - People driving on the expressway differently than you do
  - A colleague asking a ridiculous question near the end of a staff meeting

Once you identify a trigger, use it as a mental cue to take a few mindful breaths and shift your focus to the experience. For example, if you stop at a red light, rather than thinking, "I should have gone. I need to get where I'm going," take a slow, deep breath. Focus on the air entering your lungs. Let your senses do their thing. You can also nonjudgmentally note whatever emotion you're feeling, as in "I realize I'm feeling anxious to get to work."

When you breathe, do so intentionally and slowly. Feel the air fill the bottom of your lungs first, lifting your stomach. Then focus on air filling up your lungs as your chest rises. Hold the breath for a few seconds. Then reverse the exhale, letting go of the air at the top of your throat, followed by your chest, then belly.

One byproduct of this mindful moment is the activation of our *parasympathetic nervous system*, which dampens our stress response (Jerath, 2006). Most people are familiar with the "fight-or-flight" response, which is triggered by the parasympathetic system's opposite: the *sympathetic nervous system*. When we experience (or think about) something unpleasant, the sympathetic nervous system kicks in, cuing the release of more cortisol, a stress hormone.

So, rather than having a jammed copy machine trigger rumination and fight-or-flight mode, we can use the experience to trigger a few deep, mindful breaths to activate the "rest-and-digest" mode via the parasympathetic system.

Assignment #2:
Schedule Unwired Time

My name is Chase, and I have an addiction. I'm addicted to my phone. I find myself subconsciously reaching for it and then absent-mindedly flipping through apps, checking my e-mail, checking social media sites over and over again. I used to catch myself multiple times a day getting stuck in an app-addiction cycle. I started to break the cycle with a simple approach: I scheduled some unwired, mindful time.

I now have a rule I try to follow each day. When I get home from work, I put my phone out of sight. I work to engage my attention on being present with my family. And when I go into autopilot and pat my pocket looking for my phone, I remind myself to be aware of what I'm experiencing in the moment.

Just as we sometimes need to schedule time to hang out with our friends, we can schedule time to hang out with the present moment. Whether it's five minutes or five hours, find time to disconnect from devices that divide your awareness.

Want to know just how important it is that you schedule unwired time? Enable a phone-usage app for a week. Prepare to be shocked.

Assignment #3: Meditate

If you *do* want to take mindfulness to the next level, look into practicing mindfulness meditation. Choosing from among the many programs available can be overwhelming, but the variety provides a lot of options. Much like physical fitness programs, you can find "mindful fitness" programs for any time commitment, level, and cost.

Types and costs. Different types of mindfulness programs may provide different benefits. Here's a list of categories and benefits, based on a study of 200 participants (Newman, 2017):

- **Presence**—Breathing meditations and body scans
  - Best for improving attention
- **Perspective**—Meditations that involve observing thoughts and becoming less reactive to them
  - Help regulate emotion to stay calm under stressful situations
- **Affect**—Emotional-attachment meditations such as "loving kindness"
  - Help regulate emotion and can promote compassion and altruism

Meditation programs. Here are a few examples of the many mindfulness meditation programs that are available:

- **MBSR-Umass** (https://www.umassmed.edu/cfm/)—One of the most highly researched and thorough programs is the eight-week Mindfulness-Based Stress Reduction (MBSR) program from the University of Massachusetts. For those who don't have access to an MBSR class, MBSR offers detailed online courses.

- **Mindful Schools** (www.mindfulschools.org)—For a more education-specific focus, check out Mindful Schools, featuring different levels and durations of programs. There are even options to earn CEUs. These courses are a fraction of the cost of MBSR.

- **Palouse Mindfulness** (www.palousemindfulness.com)—Dave Potter took his training from MBSR onto the internet, creating Palouse Mindfulness. If you like the words *free* and *unscheduled*, take a look at this option.

Apps. You can also find plenty of apps with guided meditations and support. Here are some to consider:

- Insight Timer—a buffet of guided meditations
- Aura—a 3-minute, personalized, daily guided meditation
- Headspace—a 10-minute-a-day guided program with a buddy-system option
- Calm—another collection of guided meditations

Although apps are a good option for the time-strained teacher, keep in mind that an app is only a resource. Just as an app can't replace a high-quality teacher in education, an app can't replace instruction from a reputable, research-based mindfulness program.

Movement-based programs. If you like to move while you practice mindfulness, consider a program that has elements of mindful breathing and focus, such as yoga, tai chi, or Pilates. Join that colleague who won't stop inviting you to a local class or scour the web for resources.

Assignment #4: Practice "Raisin Awareness"

When are you likely to be *least* mindful? When you're eating. No doubt you've had that moment when you've looked into a bag and thought, "Uh... did I really put down a half-bag of corn chips?" Yes. You probably did.

Try the mindful-eating experience. First, choose a food. Many mindfulness maestros recommend a raisin. I use an orange because (1) oranges are delicious, (2) I can use all the vitamin C I can get, and (3) they provide a rich multisensory experience for a mindfulness novice. Next, find an environment free of distractions. I also recommend doing this alone, otherwise you will feel (and look) like a weirdo. The goal is to slow down the experience of eating, focusing on each sense individually:

- **Touch and sight.** Use your fingers to examine the food thoroughly. Notice every variation and what makes it unique. Bring your attention to the actual contact points on your fingers as you notice the texture and temperature.
- **Smell.** Let the scent waft into your nostrils. Feel the sensation from the moment you notice the odor in the air through the scent traveling into your lungs.
- **Taste.** Focus on each bite and the various points of the experience: the feel of your teeth sinking in; the movement across your taste buds and under your teeth; the development of flavors; even the preparation of your swallowing reflex and how it feels when you bring that grub down to meet your stomach.

Any time your mind wanders to other thoughts (e.g., "I hope no one is watching me"), note them and bring your awareness back to the experience.

Assignment #5:
Visualize Comic Clouds

Everything we do happens through the lens of a mood or an emotional state, which makes it hard to detach our experiences from our emotions. Most mindfulness gurus recommend noting thoughts and emotions as if they were in a cloud and then watching the cloud drift away in our mind. Noting. Drifting. Noting. Drifting.

When I first tried this strategy, I felt cartoonish. I began imagining myself in a comic strip (X-Men–like on a good day, Charlie Brown–like on a bad day), seeing myself from a third-person perspective. I would see my current experience with dialogue and thought bubbles and Morgan Freeman narrating, if the mood was fitting. The detachment might seem hokey, but there is some evidence that a third-person detachment can lower the intensity of negative affect, improve emotional regulation, and help with self-control (Moser et al., 2017; Wallace-Hadrill & Kamboj, 2016).

Assignment #6:
Take a Weather Check

In Chapter 3, I discuss how the weather cues us to make mental comparisons: we instantly attach an evaluation to weather. We look out the window and either feel great because it's precisely how we want it or we get grouchy because it's not meeting our expectations.

Instead of wasting thoughts on what the weather *could* or *should* be, shift to a mindful awareness. Use the conditions outside to trigger a mindful moment. When you step into rain, take a few seconds to feel the sensations of the raindrops hitting your skin, to smell the damp soil. When the sun is blazing, feel the warmth on your skin and notice the hazy sky in the distance. In the winter, note the feel of icy air and melting snowflakes. Use the weather to practice mindful awareness.

Your mind is a classroom. It's filled with dozens of thoughts waving for your attention. But you have a choice. Do you let the thoughts run wild, or do you learn to manage them? Do you study them, or do you ignore them? Pursuing mindful awareness is like pursuing masterful teaching. It takes practice and time. But it's worth every effort.

We're not doomed to a life of rumination and rambling simply because we're teachers with a lot to think about. Nor are we destined to disappointment by the regrets of yesterday, the distance of tomorrow, or the contrast of what *is* to what *could* be. With mindful awareness, we can find fulfillment in every second we are awake, every breath we breathe, and every step we take.

Attitude: Gratitude

Happiness is not about what the world gives you....
Happiness is what you think *about what the world gives you.*

—Mo Gawdat

The internet went nuts on August 21, 2017, when the "Great American Solar Eclipse" swept our sky. Since 1918, there hadn't been a complete eclipse visible to the entire contiguous United States. People prepared months in advance, snagging eclipse glasses from libraries and websites.

I was not one of those people. I had to go about this eclipse the old-school way via a cereal box rigged with foil, a couple holes, and some tape.

Foil for reflecting disappointment

CEREAL FLAKES

Miracle of nature enters here

Eyehole

I sat for an hour in my backyard, waiting for this miracle of obstruction to blow my mind. I didn't see much initially, other than my neighbor bopping across her lawn with her own cereal box contraption. Then, the sky darkened. It was time.

Maneuvering my *Leave It to Beaver*–era device, I awaited the magic of the cosmos, ready to burst into tears at the ethereal wonder I wouldn't see again in my lifetime. And then... a microscopic light hazed for a few seconds in the cereal box and it was over. The lackluster Great American Solar Eclipse was done.

I've had a lot of disappointing moments in my life, but that solar eclipse is near the top for biggest letdowns. It didn't help that across the web, people posted *National Geographic*–caliber photos and reflections of their joy.

I couldn't be mad at the moon and the sun or the World Wide Web. Objectively, that eclipse was phenomenal. But *subjectively* I felt disappointed. Reality didn't meet my unrealistic expectations.

Our well-being suffers when we feel disappointment—not just with hyped-up eclipses, but with our students, our meals, our relationships, ourselves—even our daily weather. See for yourself: go outside and notice how you feel about the weather. This may not work as well in every state, but in Michigan, where I live, rarely is a day not too cold, too warm, too humid, too overcast, too rainy. Michigan weather may not be good for making reliable plans, but it's great for showing how much Michiganders, and people in general, love to complain about what *could* have been.

The weather doesn't dictate our happiness. How we *perceive* the weather does. If the reality meets our expectations, we're content. But if there's even a slight mismatch, we get moody. I'm not talking about severe droughts or devastating hurricanes—those obviously affect our happiness. I'm talking about the simple weather patterns that people moan about. Raining? *Ugh! Why can't it be sunny?* Sunny? *It's too hot and dry!* Snow? *Crystallized water demons!*

How much of our happiness is a choice of comparing what *is* to what *could* be? In Chapter 1 we looked at the fallibility of perception and how we choose to look for good or bad. In this chapter, we look through a different lens: How do we compare our perception of *reality* to our *expectations*? How does this comparison affect our well-being? And, what can we do to shift our attitude and make comparisons that help us—and everyone around us—thrive? We start by looking at something called "mental contrasting" and how it is demonstrated in an experience that rarely matches our expectations: traffic.

Mental Contrasting

Consider this scenario: You're behind schedule getting ready for work. You're exhausted and flustered and don't want to be late. As you drive, the stars align to cue a perfect storm of travel impairments: slow-moving vehicle in front of you; road construction closing a lane; dude who needs a few miles to figure out if he's *really* ready to turn or not. At your wits' end, seconds away from getting to work, you see the last traffic light switch to yellow. You're ready to floor the pedal and plow through the light when the car ahead of you hesitates, then makes it through the light as it turns red. You stop. You're going to be late. What thoughts run through your mind?

In moments like this, we play a remarkable (and instant) game of mental gymnastics: we compare *what is* to *what could have been*. In cognitive psychology, this game is known as *mental contrasting*.

We mentally contrast all the time, sometimes to reflect and learn, sometimes to motivate ourselves to change behavior. But a critical question for our well-being is *to what* do we compare the situation—how it could have been worse, or how it could have been better?

Upward Contrasting: Undermining Our Well-Being

In the scenario just described, you no doubt compared your circumstance to how it could have been better. The road construction could have been finished. That light could have stayed green. You could have made it to work on time. This style of contrasting is called *upward contrasting*. Think of "up" as comparing to how something could be better. More often than not, upward contrasting cues grouchiness, regret, and disappointment. It's the classic "grass is greener on the other side." In other words, upward contrasting is usually not good for our well-being.

Upward contrasting isn't just a product of near-accidents in traffic. We can see how it trounces well-being in another context that is all the rage these days (sometimes literally): social media.

There's been a lot of talk about social media being the bane of society and happiness. But the use of social media isn't the problem; the issue is that use of social media exposes our knack for upward comparisons.

In 2017, the social media app Snapchat—popular with teens, selfie lovers, and creeps of all kinds—revealed a new feature: the Snap Map. A user can pull up a map showing nearby events as well as where one's friends are, down to their specific addresses. Lauded by the company as a way to help people connect, users didn't shower the Snap Map with praise. Rather than helping folks feel linked, it cued upward comparisons as users felt left out of all the cool things they could be doing with friends. Snarky memes quickly criticized the downside of Snap Maps: "Thanks to the new Snapchat update, you can know when your friends don't invite you somewhere!"

The Snap Map demonstrates a paradox of social media: rather than boosting our well-being through connection, social media can fuel regret through upward comparisons. Generally, social media are supposed to help people connect and reap the benefits of positive relationships. Quality relationships are a major factor for well-being; however, social media can stir more social envy than engagement through upward comparisons. There's even a label for the unpleasant emotion cued by the Snap Map: FoMO, or Fear of Missing Out.

FoMO is the experience of feeling disconnected when seeing pictures of others having fun in our absence. We may be having a great day, but once we see that all our friends are living it up at that wedding we couldn't attend, our happiness gets a tinge of sadness. It isn't that our day was objectively (or even subjectively) bad. But when we see others having fun, we may feel disappointment and think, "I could be having *more* fun if I were there."

Studies are finding that social media often *diminish* our well-being. But there's a key caveat to consider: it isn't that the whole of social media destroys our well-being. Social media can, in fact, boost well-being, such as by helping elderly users communicate with relatives (Sims, Reed, & Carr, 2016). But when a study finds social media reducing our happiness, it usually isn't because of the medium itself; it's because of our upward comparisons (Appel, Gerlach, & Crusius, 2016; Verduyn, Ybarra, Résibois, Jonides, & Kross, 2017).

Consider this scenario. You scroll through your social media feed and see carefully crafted photos and updates designed to give good impressions and get "likes." Seeing others at their best—traveling the world, looking great, vying for "parent of the year"—may trigger that upward comparison. You think, "I don't remember the last time I left my zip code... I could lose a couple pounds... my kid ate a rock and broke stuff all day." You may even be prompted to boost your mood by posting your own wittiest update or photogenic pic, adding to the envy cycle.

Social media is not our foe (nor necessarily our friend). It simply cultivates more opportunities for us to make upward comparisons. To salvage our well-being, we don't need to ban social media from our lives. We need to be conscious of and vigilant against such comparisons. *Upward contrasting undermines our well-being.*

And it doesn't proliferate only on the road or online. Education provides ample opportunities to compare every aspect of how our job could be better. We pit schools against each other when discussing student progress. We compare our classrooms to our colleagues'. In our spare time, we scroll social media and online bulletin boards, noting every perfectly decorated classroom and viral teacher video. We even hold our "glory class" of yesteryear as a yardstick against which no other class could measure. If only I had *X* instead of *Y*. If only this kid knew how to solve for *X* instead of cry.

Downward Contrasting: Shifting from Disappointment to Appreciation

Although upward comparisons might be our default, here's the beautiful thing about having a cerebral cortex: we can choose to shift our attitude any time we want. We can choose to *contrast downward*, noting how a situation could be worse and how fortunate we are.

For example, let's replay that traffic scenario. Same start: You're running late, demons of delay attacking from all angles. The car ahead hesitates, then goes. For a split-second you consider running the red. Instead you slam your brakes. You're going to be late. Only this time, the car that ran the yellow light comes a split-second from getting smashed by a car coming the other way. Had you gone, you would have been sideswiped. What thoughts run through your mind this time?

When things could have been worse—like when we almost have a car accident—we may automatically contrast downward. Rather than getting grumpy about our decision, we feel thankful. We may even murmur a thank-you to our inanimate braking system or that road construction for delaying our demise. *Downward contrasting shifts us from disappointment to appreciation.*

You might be thinking, "Well, duh. Of course I'd be more appreciative if I avoided an accident." But what about less severe situations? Although our brains might automatically kick into an upward comparison in certain situations, we can still switch to a downward comparison. We're not slaves to our automatic responses (which is why we're able to say no to other impulses, like eating entire pizzas by ourselves).

This point is critical: we can *choose* to contrast downward as easily as we choose to contrast upward. I can therefore choose to be grateful, to boost my well-being, rather than choose to be disappointed and undermine my happiness. When I'm grouchy because my Wi-Fi crashed for a few minutes, I can choose to reframe: at least I exist at a time when instant access to a lifetime of information and entertainment is the *norm*. When I'm stuck in traffic, I can choose to consider how lucky I am to have the financial means to use transportation. When I look at the roster of rowdy students on my new class schedule, I can choose to contrast downward: at least I have a chance to change the life of someone who really needs it.

It's critical to point out that downward comparisons have limitations. We shouldn't compare to how a situation could be worse in every instance. For example, when there's social injustice, saying "It could be worse" is a recipe for destructive complacency. Or, if you're trying to shift some eating habits and find yourself scarfing down that third "stress donut," it might not be motivating to think, "At least I'm not eating three sticks of butter."

We also shouldn't try to trigger downward contrasting in others. There's a reason why the saying "There are other fish in the sea" usually makes us want to punch a fish (or a person) in the face instead of boosting our mood.

But consider those moments when choosing a downward comparison could reframe your well-being. Last winter I recall taking my garbage out in subzero temperatures. Despite the whole trip taking less than 10 seconds, I griped about the misery of the cold. I realized I was upward contrasting. So I flipped the thought process. Some people don't have the luxury of warm clothes. It could be worse. Some don't have a warm home, a warm bed to return to. It could be worse. In a 10-second trip, I had taken for granted so many fortunate things about my life. A flip of my mental attitude from an upward comparison of disappointment to a downward comparison of appreciation made an instant change in my level of contentment.

Used strategically, downward contrasting cushions us from a dip in our satisfaction. But making this switch does more than keep us from being disappointed in life. *Downward contrasting triggers gratitude, which is one of the most researched and influential positive emotions at our disposal, capable of transforming our well-being.*

Consider Thanksgiving—for some people in the United States, the Thanksgiving holiday, with its obligatory expressions of gratitude, is the only time they think much about what they have to be thankful for—and then, only fleetingly. Unfortunately, stale statements on Thanksgiving Day underrepresent the immense influence gratitude can have on our lives. Studies have found that expressing gratitude to others strengthens relationships (Lambert, Clark, Durtschi, Fincham, & Graham, 2010). It predicts better sleep, even independent of other factors such as neuroticism (Wood, Joseph, Lloyd, & Atkins, 2009). It may protect us from illness (Mills et al., 2015). Important for the world of educators, it has even been found to reduce burnout in teachers (Chan, 2011).

And if you think that trying to boost our own happiness with gratitude is selfish, give pause: gratitude increases and drives our prosocial behavior, even that of helping strangers (Bartlett & DeSteno, 2006). Most of all, gratitude is not just correlational; ample studies have shown that intentional actions of gratitude, such as writing down blessings or expressing gratitude to others, has an immediate and lasting impact on our well-being (Emmons, 2007).

What makes gratitude remarkable is that it can come in so many different forms. From our Empowered Thriving Model, presented in the Introduction to this book, we can see that gratitude can be an awareness, an attitude, and an action.

As an *awareness*, we can take the time to notice fortunate things in our lives, such by as looking for something good that happened to us today. We can also choose to shift our *attitude* to be more grateful, like switching from a complaint about spilling our latte (upward contrast) to being thankful that the break room has a coffee pot to replenish us (downward contrast). Also, gratitude can be something we express through our words or objects— transforming it into a "gift" we give or an *action* we take. Gratitude is the Triple Crown of well-being.

Gratitude goes even deeper than helping us reframe our thoughts; it builds connection. Robert Emmons (2007), a guru on the topic, identifies two components of gratitude: (1) acknowledging good things in our lives and (2) recognizing the contributions of others. The first component alone is helpful to our well-being, enhancing our goodness curator awareness. But the second part can take our happiness and relationships to the next level.

In addition to helping us appreciate our lives more, gratitude illuminates the power of human relationships and the necessity of being good to others. Rarely, if ever, does a feeling of gratitude end egocentrically. The very nature of feeling grateful is realizing that other things and people have brought us good fortune. We can feel appreciative toward a multitude of sources: people in our lives, spiritual beings, even individuals across the world we will never see.

I might get salty about a day at work and then contrast downward to shift my attitude, realizing that I'm fortunate to have a job where I make a difference. I've acknowledged something good, but gratitude leads me deeper. I didn't just wake up one day with a job. I was hired by a person (or group) who gave me a chance. I was educated by countless teachers and mentors to get to a place of competence. I'm even grateful for the car, designed and built by hundreds of strangers, that got me to the interview. I could trace dozens if not hundreds of other people who helped bring this good thing into my life, even folks I've never met.

When we experience gratitude, we connect more profoundly with our lives and the people around and before us. And when we realize others have helped us, we're inspired to pay it forward—to not merely *feel* good, but *do* good. Gratitude creates ripples of goodness and meaning.

To become a thriving educator, minimizing upward contrasting is step one. Practicing downward contrasting is step two. Step three is recognizing our deep connection to the many things in our lives for which we should be grateful. Let's scroll through some assignments.

Life Assignments

Ironically, we often need to remind ourselves to practice gratitude—to pull ourselves from upward comparisons into downward comparisons. One of my favorite ways to hold myself accountable and build more grateful habits is to practice "Gratituesday." Each Tuesday (or any day), take on one of the following assignments.

Assignment #1: Count Blessings

The most familiar and widely used gratitude intervention is the gratitude journal, which has a strong track record for boosting well-being, even weeks and months after the intervention (Emmons, 2007). In clinical settings, gratitude journals are often as effective as other rigorously tested and trusted interventions (Wood, Froh, & Geraghty, 2010). Most of all, the practice of keeping a gratitude journal is simple and quick.

Here's the instruction: *Once a day, write down a few things for which you are grateful.* You can be specific, as in this example: "I'm thankful that student told me my fly was open before class started," or general, as in, "I'm thankful to come home to a loving family." Easy, right?

Despite the simplicity, there are some tips I've learned after practicing and teaching about gratitude journals for years:

- **Tip #1: Don't make it a chore.** Some studies have found that writing in the journal once a week is more beneficial than doing it daily, especially for students (Emmons, 2007). Once it's a chore, we stop feeling grateful.

- **Tip #2: One deep reflection is better than multiple shallow thoughts.** When I teach my students to write gratitude reflections, I invite them to add a "because" section. When we elaborate on why and for whom we are grateful, we deepen our appreciation and recognize other people (or beings) who positively contributed to our lives. Reflecting on "why" helps us be more mindful and thoughtful about the source of good.

- **Tip #3: It's not a pass/fail practice.** Some people have visions of diligently writing in a gratitude journal on a schedule. Habituating appreciation is a great thing, but we also know that life doesn't always follow our agenda. Don't quit the practice if you fall off your plan. Add to your journal whenever you're able—even if days or weeks pass between entries.

If you have time to post a status or picture on social media, you have time to reflect on something for which you're grateful. In fact, try replacing a social media status update with a moment of gratitude. Not only will you reduce some potential for upward contrasting and envy cycles, but you'll also take action to improve your well-being.

Assignment #2: Write a Gratitude Letter (and Pay a Visit)

I've seen my father cry twice. The man is stoic. Thirty-plus years of working construction have hardened his façade. Calloused, sandpaper hands. Limbs knocked and cracked so frequently that they seem to have superfluous joints. I once heard him scream a masterful oration of profanity as a drill bit slid through his finger. He reversed the drill, blood and sweat splotching the bathroom floor, and went back to work. Still, no tears.

The first time I saw his eyes water, he had taken a pop-fly baseball straight to the eye. I was 6 years old, and to this day I don't know if he was actually crying or if his eyes were just leaking as a defense mechanism. He went back to playing.

The second time I saw him cry, though, it was real tears. He cried because I wrote him a gratitude letter.

I had decided to take on a research-based intervention called a gratitude visit. For the visit, one writes a letter of gratitude to a person, then meets with the person to share it. Normally, the writer reads the letter out loud to the recipient. I skipped the out-loud part because my father and I don't exchange emotions much. I handed him the letter on Christmas.

I watched as he started to read the letter. A few lines in, he left the room. Minutes later, I glanced into the other room and saw tears flowing down his hardened cheeks. We hugged. We talked. And we grew. To this day, that letter was one of the most impactful things that has happened to our relationship. It helped me realize how important he was in my life. It allowed him to understand how much I loved him. And it prompted us both to set aside the challenges, the petty annoyances, and the differences that exist in a father-son relationship.

Don't let the simplicity of a gratitude visit fool you. It's a powerful intervention for well-being. I've seen and heard of its power over and over. Every year my students take on the same assignment, writing and sharing letters of gratitude. Parents frame the letters for their desks and walls. Students share stories of breaking down in authentic connection with their intimidating coaches. Friends refuse to talk about it after the exchange, afraid of choking up again. If there's one action I recommend every person try, it's the gratitude visit.

Take out some paper and start it simply with "Dear _____."
Then, write whatever comes to mind when you think of why you're grateful for this person. You can use these sentence stems as well:

- I remember when…
- I want to thank you for…
- You might not realize how…
- I will never forget…
- You have helped me…
- Because of you, I…

By writing and reflecting, you will instantly cue gratitude. But push yourself to share it. The practice of a "gratitude visit" has been shown to boost well-being more than a gratitude journal, and for up to three months later (Seligman, Steen, Park, & Peterson, 2005). Sharing your gratitude letter allows you to get another, often deeper dose of appreciation and transfer it onto someone else. You get and give gratitude. Go ahead. Put this book down and start writing.

Assignment #3: Interconnect the Dots

Every day, you mindlessly pick up your favorite pen and use it. Beyond considering its utility value, though, when is the last time you paused to think about how many lives it took to bring that everyday object into your life?

I woke up to the interconnectedness of life when I volunteered to test pen prototypes for a design company (#nerdalert). I came across an invitation for the study and decided to go for it because it paid $150. The whole experience showed me how much effort goes into things we take for granted.

I spent an hour writing with a handful of prototypes as two researchers observed every action. These dudes spent hours, possibly days, designing prototypes, setting up cameras and sensors to record my writing, and creating controlled studies—just to make a pen that most people lose or run through the washing machine without a second thought. Using a pen, then, provides more than opportunities to write. It's a chance to channel our interconnectedness to hundreds of lives that affect us. It's a chance for gratitude.

If you ever feel like you don't have something to be grateful for, then you aren't looking (or thinking) hard enough. Look around right now. Pick one random object—the book or electronic device in your hand, the chair you're sitting in. Dozens if not hundreds of people brought that thing into your life.

Interconnecting the dots is a mental reflection in which you consider all the lives that helped bring something to you. For example, I ask my students to consider the clothes they're wearing. Then I have them spend a few minutes brainstorming about all the people who brought those clothes to them. Farmers harvested the material. Then people (or machines designed and run by people) processed that material into fabric, which was then gathered and transported by other people to be sent to dyers and designers. More people crafted those designs into sewn clothing. Because of still others—bosses, parents, siblings—resources were exchanged in order to own the clothes. Any one of those roles and processes could be further broken down—the engineers who designed the transportation vehicles, the construction workers who built the facilities, the cashier at the store.

Interconnecting the dots can trigger appreciation of good things and recognition of helpful others. Whether it's a pen, a cheeseburger, or the book (or device) you're holding in your hand, you're surrounded by reasons to be grateful. You don't need to sit down and list all the people responsible for a moment or an object. Just pause occasionally and issue a silent thank-you to a few who come to mind.

Assignment #4:
Perform Mental Subtraction

Will I boost my affect more if I think about how I met my wife or what my life would be like if I *hadn't* met my wife? Is it better to think of the *presence* of good or the *absence* of good? Although we might predict that pondering the presence of good will make us happier, research shows that thinking about the absence makes the heart grow happier (Koo, Algoe, Wilson, & Gilbert, 2008).

If you're looking for a change-up in your gratitude game, after noting something good, elaborate your thoughts on how life would be different *without* that positive thing, person, or event. Psych geeks call this *mental subtraction*.

OK, right now you may be thinking, "When I think about my life without [challenging student], it's pretty sweet, actually." Sure, we can think of how life would be better minus an annoyance, but that's an upward contrast. Save your mental subtractions for downward contrasts.

In the words of Clarence Odbody, the character of ghostly fame in the movie *It's a Wonderful Life*, "Strange, isn't it? Each man's life touches so many other lives. When he isn't around he leaves an awful hole, doesn't he?" Sometimes considering life without something present helps us realize that it is a gift.

Assignment #5:
Write a Weekly Thank-You Note

Ah, the power of a sticky note. Here's a quick shout-out to Arthur Fry, the American inventor whose ingenuity combined sticky goo with little bits of paper to create one heck of a versatile office supply. I'm grateful for sticky notes not only for keeping my chaotic life somewhat organized, but for serving as a ninja-esque medium for experiencing and expressing gratitude.

Here's your challenge. Once a week, write down a note of appreciation toward a student on a sticky note. Then, at a low-key time, place it on the student's desk and walk away. It will take you 10 seconds, but it may transform your relationship with that student and deepen your sense of gratitude.

You're disqualified from this challenge, by the way, if you use the note to manage student behavior (e.g., "Thank you in advance for not interrupting other students"). Gratitude is for connecting, not controlling. If you're using gratitude as a manipulation tool, you're doing it wrong.

Assignment #6:
Cultivate a Classroom of Gratitude

Interested in taking gratitude to the next level? One of the most rewarding ways to strengthen gratitude is to teach it. Appendix A provides multiple lessons and activities to help students feel the power of gratitude in their own lives.

As I write this chapter, I can look out my window and see my neighbor's lawn. I know *exactly* where my lawn ends and his begins. His grass is actually green—lush, fertilized, watered whenever needed. Crisp, precise mower lines cross in symmetrical mastery. Then there's my lawn. The only things crisp are the dying brown patches being choked out by weeds and negligence. The grass is literally greener on the other side.

Many times I come home and "pull an upward," thinking how much better my lawn could be (it doesn't help that my dog lies exclusively in the neighbor's yard, judging and scolding me for our

scorched grass). But in those moments, I'm reminded of a statement my colleague, a veteran teacher and parent, says often: "The
grass isn't greener on the other side; the grass is greenest where
you water it."

You probably won't see me spending thousands of dollars and
dozens of hours on my grass; my time is better spent playing with
my son and loving my wife (and dog). But you will see me watering my life by giving it the attention it deserves—paying attention
to the many things for which I should be grateful, the many ways
in which life could be worse, the many people whose actions make
life worth living.

Education can be a thankless job. We can long for other classrooms, contexts, and sometimes even other careers, upwardly
comparing to how it could be better. We can choose to neglect
our lawn. Or we could water it with gratitude. Our lives and our
careers are filled with good fortune. Are we looking hard enough?

Attitude: Finite Framing

Live as if you'll die tomorrow; learn as if you'll live forever.

—Unknown

Teachers are obsessive people. Fresh dry erase markers and clean whiteboards. Perfect lines and symmetry. Papers turned in without that frilly spiral-bound-notebook fuzz. *Your* and *you're* and *their, there, they're*. We get obsessed with details, small and large. But there's one thing we obsess about more than anything else: the future.

We obsess about the future in the "children are our future" sense, pondering how our kids will become productive citizens and people of integrity. We obsess about the future in the curricular sense, planning for the next unit, the next assessment, the next day. We even obsess about the future in the immediate sense, diligently crafting the next Jedi-ninja-wizard trick to influence student understanding. This obsession is a part of the territory. Our entire occupation is about transforming today's pupils into tomorrow's makers and shakers.

But what if the very focus of our profession—thinking about the future—impairs our sense of purpose? Our fascination with the future comes at a cost to our sense of meaning. By constantly thinking about what's next, we lose sight of what's *now*. We become obsessed, reliant on future potentials to fulfill our goals. We link our sense of happiness and purpose to a distant *when*. I call this destructive obsession with the future "when-ism."

We practice when-ism whenever we hitch our emotional well-being to a specific event or moment that we aren't currently experiencing. Basically, it's whenever we think or say, "I'll be happy when...." Consider these examples:

- I'll be happy when I retire.
- How long until he stops talking? I'll be thrilled to get out of this conversation.
- If I got a raise, then I would be content.
- Once it's Friday, I'll be on cloud 9.
- If Kurt doesn't show up to class today, I'll be *ecstatic*.

Sure, Kurt not showing up to class would make life easier; there's a chance Kurt is single-handedly ruining our lives. But this practice of when-ism creates a cycle of languishing.

Because of our obsession with the future, we spend our weeks, days, and hours considering what skill we haven't taught yet, what e-mails we need to get to, what tests we need to grade. The practice that helps us plan ahead keeps us from recognizing the powerful, purposeful experiences existing in our present.

When-ism is a product of our lack of mindfulness. When we focus on future happiness, we stop paying attention to things in the present that could be sources of happiness. In Chapter 2 we explored the value of being fully present from the perspective of reducing stress. Now we take the concept deeper to see how shifting our awareness of the present transforms our source of meaning.

When-ism matters because of the huge assumptions attached to it. When we attach our well-being to "later," we assume that another day, another chance, another moment is guaranteed. *It's not*. We assume we'll have tomorrow to begin being happy. *We might not*.

Time is no guarantee. The beauty and tragedy of life is that it is fragile. Sometimes it takes a catastrophic life experience to jolt us out of when-ism and help us wake up to the reality of impermanence.

I woke up to this reality after a conversation I had when I was 15. It would take years before the importance of the conversation anchored my life, but that conversation has brought more meaning to my life than any other. Let me paint the scene.

It's the summer before sophomore year in high school. I'm in that dreaded yet necessary rite called "driver training." Class has released and I'm just loafing around, waiting for my mom to pick me up. The minute hand has spun around. I'm still waiting, throwing a silent, personal pity party. My hormonal angst is rising. And then I notice that only one other kid is still waiting: Daniel.

Though I had shared classes with Daniel for years, I had never talked to him. He was not the most extroverted kid. I can't blame him, though. He was frequently bullied because he didn't dress or act the part of the preferred social hierarchy of school. But I knew something about him—something tragic.

A year or so earlier, Daniel's three sisters were leaving the house in their parents' van. The oldest was driving and backing out. Some people said she reached down to grab a hairbrush. Others said she was distracted by conversation. Regardless of the cause, she pulled out of the driveway not knowing a truck was coming down the street. The truck struck the van with enough force to kill Daniel's sisters.

In a split-second, Daniel lost all his siblings.

Perhaps it was knowing Daniel's tragedy—or maybe it was avoiding boredom or being the two loners left at school—that led me to talk to him that summer. As you picture this conversation, you may see us having a deep talk about his sisters and about how he was coping. You may visualize this Hollywood moment where

Daniel and I become best buds and I bash the heads of his bullies. None of that happened. We did not become lifelong amigos. I don't remember even talking about his sisters.

I simply asked him about his life and found out about how he collects medieval swords, his love for the show *Highlander*, the uncle he's close to. And then we parted ways. It was the only conversation I ever had with him.

Two years later, Daniel was riding with his friends to the local vocational-tech center. It was typical for students to take their time eating lunch and then speed to get to the vo-tech center on time. The driver, along with Daniel and his other two friends, decided to try to jump a train track and catch air. They succeeded—and in the process the car rolled out of control, flipped, combusted, and killed all three passengers—including Daniel.

In the span of half a decade, Daniel's parents lost all their children. The enormity and depth of that tragedy is beyond my comprehension. The only thing I could comprehend was the fact that I had had one, and only one, conversation with that guy.

How can a conversation change a person's perspective, especially if it happens only once? The conversation with Daniel by itself was not the game changer for me. It was the tragedy surrounding Daniel—and my recognizing the fragility of life—that changed me. I faced two simple facts: (1) I would never get to talk to that unique human being again; and (2) I will forever be filled with regret, knowing that I should have said what I wanted to say: that I thought he was a cool kid, that I respected his courage to follow his own path, that if he ever needed someone to talk to, I could be there. But I didn't say any of that. I took a moment for granted.

That conversation with Daniel was my wake-up call. And the alarm was this: *Life is a series of finite moments.* There is no greater antidote to when-ism than realizing that each moment is finite.

Finite Framing and How It Applies to Teaching

Every moment we experience—every lesson, every conversation, every interaction—is unique. Recognizing the uniqueness of every moment helps us curb when-ism. I call this practice "finite framing." Finite framing is the mental shift required to recognize that—

- Each moment is unique.
- Each moment will end.

How do we apply finite framing to the monotony of teacher life, such as the fact that we may teach the same thing again and again? Set aside the fact that life can change dramatically in 24 hours. Even if a similar moment probably *will* happen again, a person can finite-frame because she will never experience that moment in exactly the same way again—the people, the context, the knowledge will be different tomorrow. I could teach the exact same lesson to the exact same students tomorrow, but each of us has changed in minor (or major) ways within 24 hours. The uniqueness of each moment is what makes it finite. The Greek philosopher Heraclitus rocked this idea when he said, "You could never step into the same river twice" (Durant, 1991).

Now, there are extreme versions of finite framing in which people focus *only* on the negatives of not getting a moment back. However, if all we think about is the potential doom that may strike us or our students—or if we focus only on our regret and remorse—we'll live in a mopey, weepy, hot mess. If you've ever been around someone prone to bursting into nostalgic tears, you know how awkward that gets.

Instead, finite-frame by cuing your mental dialogue to engage a healthy mental contrast. Do this by shifting *when-ism* to *what-if-ism*. To understand what-if-ism, here are a few examples. Notice how each of these thoughts cues our perspective to finite framing:

- What if I don't get another opportunity to show my appreciation?
- What if this were my last conversation with this person? Would I be happy with how I treated him?
- What if I never get to have this experience again? What can I do to make the most out of it?
- What if I don't see this person again? Do I really want to spend this moment focusing on such an insignificant thing?
- What if this person could really use some support today with some kind words?

What-if-ism prompts us to contrast downward and consider what it would be like if we lost this experience, this person, or this moment. We are, in a sense, hedging the potential for regret by finite framing to be authentic and present with others. Regret is linked to negative emotional states and lower life satisfaction (Wrosch & Heckhausen, 2002). But by finite framing, we get two benefits: we often have a better experience in the moment, and we may reduce the likelihood of regret in the future.

Finite framing doesn't have to directly involve the other person. For example, without overtly mentioning anything to my students, I can shift my attitude and remember that I will only get this one lesson, this one time, with this one set of students.

But when we finite-frame to involve others, we reap larger benefits. The best place to apply this? Conversation.

Meaningful Conversation

Students get used to unconventional lessons in our positive psychology class. But they're confused when I give them this prompt for one of my favorite lessons: "For the entire hour, you have one task: have a good conversation with your partner."

I arrange the desks in columns, paired up and angled toward each other for one-on-one conversation. With nothing more than the initial prompt, I set them loose and observe their interactions.

If you imagine yourself—or a teenager—in this situation, you can predict some likely behaviors. Protective nonverbals. Awkward silences. Cell phones checked occasionally (or constantly). One near-guarantee, though, is that the conversation will start at a similar level: shallow small talk. We can categorize conversation into one of three levels. Level 1 is Weather Talks, Level 2 is Interest Talks, and Level 3 is Meaningful Talks.

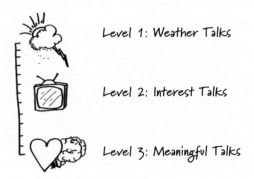

Level 1 conversations are emotionally safe and about external things like weather, sports, or television. Gossip is among the favored genres of Level 1. Almost every conversation we have with someone we don't know well—or do know well—starts at Level 1. *Can you believe this weather? Nuts, right?* Even questions that could elicit deeper responses, like "How are you?" trigger a Level 1 response. *Good. You? Good.*

Level 2 reveals some information about who we are as people—where we live or grew up, our hobbies and interests, the plot of memories. It's more revealing than Level 1 but still pretty safe emotionally. We *start* to bond at this level.

Level 3 topics show the authentic core of our identity. We discuss memories and the emotions attached—our hopes, dreams, fears, aspirations, needs. Religion. Politics. Here we are vulnerable but authentic. True connection happens here.

I ask my students to pause after some time with their partners, and we discuss the levels. Then they assess what level they were mainly at. Rarely do any partners say they made it to Level 3. Some have progressed to Level 2, but most are at Level 1, which is normal.

However, one critical part of finite framing is talking about meaningful things, being authentic, and cuing genuine curiosity about someone else. Put differently, a Level 3 conversation is finite framing in action. We don't take these conversations for granted.

Meaningful conversation is also tied to well-being. One interesting study recorded random snippets of 79 young adults' conversations, with their permission. The researchers (Mehl, Vazire, Holleran, & Clark, 2010) collected nearly 24,000 recordings and categorized them based on the level of meaning versus "small talk." Using well-being surveys, researchers found that happiness didn't just correlate with quantity of conversation. It's true that more interaction was linked with more happiness. But quality also mattered. Compared to unhappy people, happy individuals spent a third less time on small talk (what I would call Level 1) and had twice as many meaningful conversations (Level 3).

After sharing this research with my students, we define and discuss finite framing. I then challenge my students to converse at "Level 2.5," or simply try to avoid staying at Level 1. In other words, I remind them, "You will never have this conversation with this person, in this way, on this day, again in your life. Make the most of it."

I also give them examples of meaningful conversation topics tied to pleasant emotion. Sure, talking about one's worst memory is Level 3, but we don't have to go into a negative state to bond and have meaningful interaction.

At the end of the lesson and on post-course surveys, students cite this lesson as one of the most important and influential lessons taught in the class. Some students say they had a better talk with their partner than they often have with the people with whom they have their closest relationships. And many write that they established a true friendship with someone they barely knew. They find what I have found ever since my experience with Daniel: when we finite-frame a conversation and talk about meaningful things—even once—it can have profound influence on our relationships and well-being.

You don't have to have constant, deep conversation with everyone all the time. But imagine "leveling up" just 5 or 10 percent of your conversations. Do you have to gossip about students or administrators in the staff lounge, or could you ask a colleague what got her into teaching? Is "What TV show are you into?" our only option for chatting with students, or can we ask them what their favorite memory is from the year so far? Small tweaks can help us make the most of finite moments.

If you like resources, search online for one of *The New York Times*'s most popular articles: "The 36 Questions That Lead to Love" (Jones, 2015). The article is based on an experimental study in interpersonal closeness that used a host of Level 3 questions to help strangers feel emotionally close (Aron, Melinat, Aron, Vallone, & Bator, 1997). You can use the list of questions for meaningful conversation starters. (Don't worry. You can use them without the goal of falling in romantic love.)

Life Assignments

Beyond having deeper conversations, here are five other assignments for practicing finite framing and making the most of moments that happen only once.

Assignment #1:
Designate "Finite-Frame Friday"

Once a week, write a positive note expressing a thought that you've never actually said to a student, a colleague, an administrator, or a parent. Designating a specific day, such as "Finite-Frame

Friday," helps turn finite framing into a cognitive habit (we get a weekly dose of positive emotion as we express meaningful words to others) and can make the task more manageable. As teachers, we already have a lot on our plates, so finite framing can feel like another overwhelming thing to do. But we don't need to tell every person every appreciative thought we have in one sitting. We can do just one small thing—write a note, make a phone call, or send an e-mail—once a week, taking five minutes during lunch, before the workday starts, or as it ends. Having an intentional plan to express kind words also lets us avoid the regret we may feel if tragedy happens and we realize we'll never get another chance to tell someone how we feel.

The school where I teach has "pride" postcards to send home to parents, letting them know how great their kid is. We're required to submit three of these a year (yes, expressing kind words is a requirement). However, each Friday, I take five minutes during lunch to send one home. I look at my roster and think about which student has recently made me smile or done something nice for others. Rather than let those thoughts evaporate or hang on until "later," I jot them down. I call this note a triple-whammy: I get to express kind words, the parent gets to read kind words, and usually the student will hear about those kind words. Everyone's positivity gets a boost through expressing appreciation *now* instead of waiting until later.

Regardless of what plan you choose, make a small investment in time that pays meaningful dividends. Set aside time once a week to take advantage of the uniqueness of each moment.

Assignment #2: Do a "Convo-Check"

Next time you catch yourself not engaging in a conversation, prompt yourself with this question: "What if I don't get a chance to listen to this person again?"

You've undoubtedly experienced many moments when you *look* like you're having a conversation, but you're not really listening to the person doing the talking. Consider this example: You're on a frantic run to do some last-minute copying, and then that colleague comes in to shoot the breeze—the one who can talk and talk, ignoring your clear nonverbal cues of urgency. You're standing with your body practically out of the door, yet your colleague is still trying to remember the exact wording of that joke he read. Your face is sore from fake smiling and nodding. You want out.

Moments like this are fuel for when-ism. We divide our attention, thinking about how much we have to do and how this moment will be better when we're out of this conversation. Consider these moments a perfect opportunity for what I call a "convo-check." For example, think: "What if I just gave a couple focused minutes and appreciated this moment? What if I took this moment to appreciate how lucky I am to have people who want to chat with me? What if this person hasn't felt heard all day and I can *be* that person who hears him?" If these words don't work for you, think of any phrasing you can use to remind yourself to find meaning in even minor conversations.

Assignment #3:
Assign a Classroom Cue

Assign a common classroom event as a cue to remind yourself that the moment you are in will never happen again. I started doing convo-checks because I realized I had a common when-ism cue: walking into my classroom for the first time in the morning. That's when I'm thinking of 30 different things I should have planned before I left the previous day. It's also usually when a pack of students are waiting outside my door, wanting to chat with me before the bell rings. *Who are these teenage anomalies wanting to chat at 7:30 in the morning!?* After years of morning grouching and when-isms, I decided to link my morning to the convo-check. I made mornings an opportunity for mindful finite framing.

To this day, I still have tons of planning and copying to complete before my first class—and I still have students hovering around my door. But I've made each morning a "what-if" cue. I remind myself that I can have a great day regardless of whether my handouts are perfectly aligned and take a rare few minutes to just connect with students. What if these students are here each morning because they *need* someone to connect with before they journey back into those hallway jungles? What if I showed up tomorrow and those unique, caring students weren't there?

Find a moment in your day when you often go into autopilot or drift into when-ism. It might be when you're greeting students as they enter the room, turning on an overhead projector or other piece of tech equipment, waiting for the class-start bell to ring, or walking kids from one class to another. Use your classroom moment to cue a finite frame. You will have a momentary boost of meaning and engagement and repeating this cue will make finite framing your norm.

Assignment #4: Post a Quotation

Post a quotation that grabs your attention and reminds you to finite-frame. It might be a quotation that had a profound effect on your own life. For example, I don't remember who first told me this when I was younger, but at one point as I was whining about how dull my life was, someone said to me, "Only boring people get bored." Instant mind shift. I still remind myself whenever I feel bored that boredom is a state of mind and I control it.

I use quotations to help cue these mental shifts, including lines that remind me to finite-frame. What are the lines that remind you that life is fragile, that moments are unique, that a meaningful life is a product of our choices? I've embedded a few of my favorites into this chapter already, but here are a couple of others that plucked powerful chords in my mind:

- "Yesterday is gone. Tomorrow has not yet come. We have only today. Let us begin." —Mother Teresa

- "Happiness, not in another place but this place... not for another hour but this hour." —Walt Whitman
- "At the end of the day people won't remember what you said or did; they will remember how you made them feel." —Maya Angelou

Posting quotations, though, can be tricky because of how easily stimuli blend into our environment. Find a place that is novel enough to catch your attention from time to time. Here are some suggestions that have worked for me or others I know:

- On the bathroom mirror
- On the window looking out of your classroom
- Above your classroom whiteboard
- Next to your vehicle's speedometer
- On the background of your phone or computer screen
- Next to your school phone
- Big and bold on a wall of your classroom

Words have power, so use them to give power to the potential in each finite moment.

Assignment #5:
Create a "Meaning Museum"

To remind yourself to finite-frame, create a "meaning museum"—a collection of tangibles that remind you to value each moment. More specifically, collect every meaningful e-mail or note you've received from a student, a colleague, or a parent. If you've taught for a while, you've no doubt received such notes, expressing the sender's appreciation and gratitude. If you haven't taught for long, you'll get them soon. Trust me. Beyond affirming our choice to teach, these notes remind us that the small moments we take for granted have a lasting influence on others.

A drawer next to my desk contains every kind note I've received from someone along my teaching journey. These notes prove a powerful paradox: though every moment is finite and fragile, these small moments can have infinite influence on the lives around us. *This* is the heart of finite framing. Moments aren't insignificant because they're temporary; moments matter.

As I was drafting this chapter, for example, I received an e-mail from a former student. It included a video recording of a speech she gave for her college class about a person who influenced her. I can't fully describe how meaningful it was to see that recording. That girl and I had been through a *lot* over her four years in high school, including my reporting her self-harming, which she says saved her life.

I'm sure I poured dozens of extra hours into helping her—and I'm sure during those hours I more than once slipped into whenism, imagining the other many things I needed to do. But this girl, like many students, needed *someone* who would just be there, even when I had so many other "required tasks" to do.

I remember having convo-checks cuing me to be present: What if she needs this conversation to keep from hurting herself? What if this brief moment can remind her to keep believing in herself?

That video of appreciation is a testament to the importance of finite framing and investing in our minor moments. It will be a part of my meaning museum for as long as I teach (and live).

But there's more to why that video is worth keeping: the person recording that student—the professor of her college class—was also my former teacher. He was the one person who I felt invested in me, who inspired me to teach, who gave me meaningful interactions. His interactions, finite and brief, transcended an entire generation to help me help others.

Meaning museums, and the artifacts they contain, show us the ripple effects we make when we don't take our interactions for granted. Moments change lives. Collect evidence to prove that.

Life is composed of finite moments. In every interaction we can choose our internal dialogue. Are we simply waiting for what's next, zoning in on what could be better? Or are we recognizing that these small incidents are potent with meaning? *Every* moment can matter if we choose to let it, to see it, to make it so. Choose to make meaning.

Attitude: Optimism

There are two times you need to rise:
When you want to and when you don't.

—Unknown

You're undoubtedly familiar with an unrealistic analogy about a glass and some liquid:

Half Full?   Half Empty?

I say it's unrealistic for a couple of reasons. First, a constant rosy disposition is unrealistic. The "glass half full" stereotype misleads us into thinking we must be perfect. We all have rough days. They're called full-moon days, post-break days, testing days, and holiday party days. Ask me if a glass is half full or half empty on a Monday and I'll simply stare at you in a stupor. The second and more important reason why this analogy is silly is because, in teaching, how you look at a glass of liquid isn't as important as what you do with it:

Glass of Adversity

Dealing with Adversity

What influences our well-being in the classroom (and beyond) is not only how we look at normalcy but also what we do with adversity. How do we frame and respond to the everyday challenges that confront the average educator, the typical human?

We get all kinds of different "glasses" in our classrooms. Some are brimming and overflowing with emotion and energy. Others are empty and wanting. Then there are the ones with cracks and chips, the ones that tip easily, the ones filled with vinegar, and the ones that aren't glasses but Super Soakers of adolescent hormones. So what do we do with *those*—the unexpected and challenging glasses of adversity? And how does our mental dialogue when confronted with such glasses influence our well-being?

Although the glass half full/half empty analogy may not be relevant to many educators, the terms it suggests—optimism and pessimism—are critical to understand. We're focusing here on a type of optimism that has more to do with broken glasses than filled ones. Scholars define optimism differently. The stereotypical "glass half full" definition refers to having "dispositional optimism," or a positive expectation for the future and with one's endeavors (Forgeard & Seligman, 2012). There are definite advantages to looking positively to the future (and the present), and we've outlined many in Chapter 1. But there are also some disadvantages when one is overly optimistic (consider the recent housing crisis as an example).

As educators, we need more than just a positive outlook. We need the type of optimism that yields *resilience*, the second definition of optimism. We need mental optimism in response to adversity, or something known as "optimistic explanatory style." I refer to this as "practical optimism." You're at least mildly familiar with this concept if you've ever taken an ed psych class. But as a refresher, we'll review the enlightening (and twisted) tale of how electrocuting dogs helped us see optimism differently.

Optimistic Explanatory Style

The genesis of optimistic explanatory style stems from a conditioning experiment engineered by Martin Seligman and Steven Maier (Seligman, 1972). Here's the gist.

Round 1:

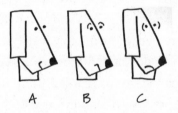

Three groups of dogs are randomly assigned to individual cages. We'll label these groups A, B, and C. If you're a dog, you want to be in Group A. Why? Because Group A dogs don't get electrocuted in Round 1. If you're not a part of puppy posse A, you want to be in Group B.

Group B gets shocked at random times, but the dogs can figure out how to work a lever or button to make it stop. Not fun, but at least controllable. Now for poor dog party C. These dogs get shocked at the exact times and for the same duration as the dogs in Group B (a practice called "yoking"). When Group B figures out a way to make the shocks stop for themselves, it also stops electrocution for Group C. If you're in Group C, your world is unpleasant chaos, and you wonder why no one asked for your consent to do this experiment.

Now for Round 2:

All the dogs are placed in new individual cages. On one end, the floor distributes random shocks. The other end is safe, though the pups need to jump over a hurdle to get there. What happens next is the detail that you no doubt discussed in your psych classes.

While dogs from Groups A and B jump to safety, many of the dogs in Group C, who were conditioned to have no control over previous shocks, sat there on the electrified end taking the jolts. Even though these canines had control over this new circumstance (they could jump over the hurdle), they gave up. This is "learned helplessness"—something you see in students who quit on challenging tests or who give up and label themselves dumb. For some, past adversities make them feel powerless in the face of new challenges.

Though the results of this groundbreaking study were fascinating, the researchers' curiosity didn't end there. They weren't narrowly focused on the dogs that learned to be helpless. They were fascinated by the dogs from Group C who *never* gave up, who still jumped the hurdle despite having no control previously (Abramson, Seligman, & Teasdale, 1978). And the interest in the persevering dogs led to studying similar resilience in humans. Many humans, despite histories of being powerless in the face of adversities, still persevere.

Factors Affecting Resilience

What are the factors affecting resilience? And how is it that some people overcome immense adversities whereas others buckle under seemingly simple annoyances? It turns out that one of the major factors affecting our ability to persevere is *not* whether we have a dispositional optimism and see the glass as half full. The key factor of resilience is explanatory, or practical, optimism—how we talk to ourselves when the glass shatters on the floor. The pattern of self-talk we use in response to adversity is our "explanatory style," and it can have massive consequences for our resilience, our accomplishment, and our well-being.

Recall that our Empowered Thriving Model involves these elements:

Awareness → Attitude → Action → Outcome

But we can do a simple swap to better understand practical optimism:

Adversity → **Attitude → Action → Outcome**

Our attitude after an adversity affects whether we take empowered action or allow powerless inaction.

An adversity is anything that doesn't go the way we want it to. Adversities can be intense or mild, ongoing or isolated. A stubbed toe is an adversity. An argument with our partner is an adversity. A failed lesson is an adversity.

We experience countless adversities throughout our day, personally and professionally. Although there are a lot of things we can do to reduce certain challenges, adversities are a part of an educator's life. So, how do we develop resilience? We examine not just the adversity, but its effect on our attitude.

Two Important Distinctions on Adversity

Although we can agree on a broad definition of adversity, it's important to acknowledge two important distinctions. First, adversities are subjective. What is a major mountain for one person is a molehill to another. For example, I once led a teacher training session at a small oil-boom town in Montana. Teachers were under major stress because their class sizes were going to double... to around 20 students.

Coming from a district where a 20-student class size would be a dream situation, I was reminded that adversity is subjective. These teachers really were under the adversities of having to double their workload, strain their resources, and revamp their classrooms.

Similarly, we need to be mindful of addressing empathy gaps with our students (something addressed in Chapter 6). To us, with our advanced knowledge and emotional security, it seems preposterous to give up on a math test after just a few errors. But to a student with developing knowledge, fear of social comparison, and an emerging sense of confidence, getting a question wrong *is* an adversity. A break-up after a one-week middle school relationship *is* an adversity to an adolescent, no matter how much we saw the end of that corny, hormonal "teen love" coming.

The second important distinction about adversity is that, despite the subjectivity of a hardship, some challenges can have a lasting impact on a person's well-being and development. On one hand, the human emotional system is pretty resilient. Hedonic adaptation—the tendency to return to an emotional set point—is a common occurrence. Studies have found that people often adapt well to major challenges like physical injuries and divorces. On the other hand, some adversities, like losing a job, can carry over the long term—even after one regains employment (Clark, Diener, Georgellis, & Lucas, 2003). We also can't ignore the long-term influence of major trauma in an adolescent's life. Multiple studies confirm that having more adverse childhood experiences (ACEs) increases an individual's risk of criminality, psychosis, physical health ailments, and mental illness (Danese & McEwan, 2012; Varese et al., 2012).

So, optimistic framing does not mean ignoring or down-playing adversities. It is not the sole tool for addressing systemic issues like unemployment and poverty cycles. I instead focus in this chapter on using practical optimism to combat the mild and moderate adversities in an educator's day-to-day life.

After Adversity

Educators are in the business of shifting beliefs. We coach students all the time on their self-talk, knowing that attitudes become actions and actions change lives. Think about a student who says, "I'm just not a math person." I can see you twitching even as you read that statement. We develop a slew of statements and strategies to help a "non-math person" reframe that mindset. But we don't often think about our style of thinking as teachers and how it affects our actions and well-being.

For example, imagine students enter your classroom just after lunch. They're yelling, running, ignoring your requests. As soon as this post-lunch party kicks off, your self-talk starts venting about *why* this adversity is happening. Which of the following statements are you more likely to think?

1. My students are always out of their minds after lunch.
2. I'm horrible at classroom management.
3. This group is wound up today.

Notice how none of these is a "glass half full" statement. I doubt any teacher is thinking, "I'm so thankful for these spirited youths knocking over chairs. Hooray for adolescence!" Instead, each of these beliefs is a different response to, or explanation of, the same adversity. Although it might not look like there's much of a difference between them, the first response is more "explanatory optimistic" than the others. The second response is the most "explanatory pessimistic" (which I'll explain in a bit). Research shows that the style of your thinking in response to an adversity can have profound influence on the actions you take (Seligman, 2011).

After decades of studying the effects of self-talk, researchers have found that practical optimism is not just another "think positive" claim of hocus-pocus self-inflation. Developing optimistic responses to adversities yields statistical benefits.

For example, imagine your phone rings. You notice the unknown number on your caller ID. You hesitate. Then you answer the call. *Hello, I'm so-and-so calling on behalf of blah-blah-blah. I was wondering if I could take a few minutes of your time.* Your inner curmudgeon creeps from the basement of your brain. You blurt a terse response before hanging up on the poor chap still talking. You go on with your day.

But what about that telemarketer? What does he do? If you've spent even a few minutes empathizing with the person on the other end of that call, you can imagine the amount of daily adversity cold-callers face: rude comments, hang-up after hang-up. Why don't they give up?

Well, many of them do give up, but some don't (kind of like those dogs from the learned helplessness study). Sales positions like telemarketing are notorious for job attrition, leading bosses to wonder how to hire resilient sales folk. Although many measures have been used to identify resilient sales people, such as education level and IQ, one well-known study found that one of the biggest predictors of who would persevere and succeed is how optimistic a person is in response to adversity.

Researchers surveyed nearly 100 salespeople from MetLife Insurance, identifying their pessimistic or optimistic explanatory style (Seligman & Schulman, 1986). They then tracked their sales and retention levels. The folks in the top half of the explanatory-style scale (i.e., the more optimistic salespeople) made 37 percent more sales than those in the bottom half. An additional study found that, of 103 new hires, the optimists made more in sales and remained in their job at twice the rate of the pessimists. Since these initial studies, others have confirmed that, if an employer is debating between two equally competent salespeople, the one with the optimistic explanatory style is the better choice (Corr & Gray, 1995).

What about sports? Studies show that during tough games, such as when a team is losing, optimists outperform pessimists as measured by objective standards like pass completion and accuracy (Gordon, 2008). Scientists have even engineered adversities by giving false feedback to swimmers and basketball players, telling them that their performance was worse than it really was. In response, pessimists' performance declines, whereas optimists maintain their skills (Martin-Krumm, Sarrazin, Peterson, & Famose, 2003; Seligman, Nolen-Hoeksema, Thornton, & Thornton, 1990).

If you couldn't care less about sports and business, consider something like, say, living a healthy life. Researchers assessed the explanatory style of 702 patients undergoing knee surgery. Two years later, the pessimists were twice as likely to report pain and half as likely to report improvement (Singh, Obyrne, Colligan, & Lewallen, 2010). A 35-year longitudinal study found that pessimists were in worse health at ages 45 to 60 as reported by doctors, even after controlling for physical health at age 25 (Peterson, Seligman, & Vaillant, 1988). Meta-analyses have also identified pessimistic style as strongly correlated with depression (Gladstone & Kaslow, 1995).

Most important to you, the educator, is the link between pessimistic responses and poorer well-being. A 2016 study of nearly

1,400 teachers found that pessimistic style is a strong underpinning for burnout and depression in educators (Bianchi & Schonfeld, 2016).

The studies cited are a few of *many* demonstrating that pessimistic self-talk can have sweeping, measurable effects on one's well-being, resilience, and performance. Which leads us to a key question: Can anything be done to change our explanatory style?

The answer is yes. One of the most consistently studied psychological interventions is cognitive behavioral therapy (CBT), which is a process of analyzing self-talk and shifting thought patterns to improve mental well-being. Shifting pessimistic thoughts to a more optimistic style is one major method of CBT. Research is robust on CBT, showing its effectiveness in reducing depression and affecting a whole host of psychiatric disorders (Butler, Chapman, Forman, & Beck, 2006; Seligman et al., 1988).

This chapter is in no way intended to serve as a substitute for legitimate cognitive behavioral therapy. So if you're feeling some strong depression or anxiety, find a professional therapist. However, for minor and moderate adversities, practicing the basics of thought shifting can be helpful. With an awareness of what to look for and diligent practice, it's possible to shift from pessimistic attitudes to optimistic attitudes.

The Twin Sins of Pessimism

When it comes to attitude style (optimistic or pessimistic), we should pay attention to two spectrums: *permanent* versus *temporary* and *universal* versus *specific*. Each attitude spectrum has a "sin" at one end. On the first spectrum, it's permanence, and on the second, it's universalization. To build our teaching resilience, we must be vigilant against these twin sins.

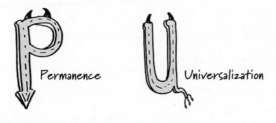

Sin #1: Permanence

The first continuum of attitude style is the extent to which you think of an adversity as permanent (pessimistic) versus temporary (optimistic). The more permanent your belief about an adversity, the less likely it is that you'll take positive action. Take the awkward experience called "dating" as an example.

You go out on a date with a very attractive person. Things seem to be going great, and you go on that visual time-hop, imagining your future together. But then something goes awry, and the person ignores your invitation for a second date. Bam! Adversity.

If your belief style is more permanent, you might think, "I always screw up good things," "I guess I'll just be lonely forever," or "I'm never going to have dual income." That belief style isn't likely to lead to the positive action of getting back out into the dating jungle. Instead, you'll probably sulk and binge on ice cream, watching depressing TV shows in the dark. If you do land some future dates, you might even carry that "permanent" adversity with you, constantly focusing on all the things that could go wrong again.

Permanent explanatory styles debilitate action by prematurely accepting defeat. This statement is just as true in the classroom as it is in the dating world. Think of a teacher who resigns to permanence, thinking:

- There's nothing I can do to help these kids be better readers.

- These kids are always horrible after lunch.
- I'll never be able to manage this group.

On the opposite end of the continuum is seeing these same adversities in a temporary light. Compare the above statements to these:

- It's going to take some strategic work to improve these kids' reading skills.
- These kids are wound up today.
- I'm struggling right now to figure out how to manage this group.

Notice, first of all, how none of these revised beliefs are "everything is great" thoughts of false optimism. Second, notice how all of these beliefs are just as—if not more—factual than the former beliefs.

As a teacher, then, you're capable of either the attitude that there's nothing you can do to help kids become better readers or that it's going to take some hard work. One thought might give you an excuse to give up, whereas the other might help you rally to find new solutions, approach the adversity from a different angle, and learn in the process.

How do you spot a permanent thought? The main clue is to look for a class of keywords that some people call "absolutes," others call "lightning words," and I call "words for derailing into an argument with my wife." Here they are:

- Never
- Always
- Every time
- Every
- Nothing

Look for these words and other patterns of permanence and delete them from your mental monologues.

Sin #2: Universalization

The second attitude continuum explores universal beliefs (pessimistic) versus specific beliefs (optimistic). A universal belief takes the adversity and generalizes it across other aspects of experience. Conversely, a specific belief pinpoints the exact cause or effect of an adversity. Whereas a failed date can highlight a permanent explanatory style, another context shows us the prevalence of universalizing adversity: sports.

Every state has a college rivalry. I can't speak for your state, but I know in Michigan, people lose their minds over the annual Michigan versus Michigan State football game. For weeks leading up to this game, houses swear allegiance with green-and-white or maize-and-blue flags, family members turn against each other, students obnoxiously trash-talk in class. As I care nothing about this game, I rarely pay attention. Yet one game lives in my memory. And it actually isn't one game—it's one play from one game. Not only is it a play that lives on in glory or infamy, depending on your point of view, but it shows just how likely someone is to adopt a universal belief about adversity.

Michigan State at Michigan, October 17, 2015. Michigan is winning the game 23-21. They have the ball and it's fourth down and two. There are 10 seconds left in the game, so Michigan plays the safe bet and decides to punt. The ball gets snapped a little low and the punter fumbles it. Not great, but at this point he really needs to do only one thing: dive onto the ball and take the down. Nope. He tries to pick it up and punt it again, a bad move when a wall of linebackers is charging you. Michigan State players smash the punter, retrieve the ball, and rush into the end zone for a game-winning touchdown. And people go nuts in the best and worst possible ways.

What has always fascinated me about sports moments like these is the adversity of a single play being universalized toward the outcome of an entire game. A team's downfall gets placed on the tragic mistake of a single player, in this case the punter causing a loss. I saw similar resignations of universal responsibility from soccer players I used to coach. "My mistake cost us the game." "If I hadn't missed that shot, we would have won."

But that's an alternative reality to the adversity, because no *single* play loses a game, and most sports aren't just a single play. A series of adversities leads to a loss. One could argue—with factual support—that the mishandled Michigan punt was one of many factors that caused a loss. For example, had other adversities not happened, Michigan would be ahead by more than a couple points. Had other adversities not happened, Michigan wouldn't be in a fourth-down situation with seconds to go. And yet, one adversity gets pessimistically universalized to a much larger scale.

We see this situation with students. Say a student is struggling with a reading passage and quips, "I just hate reading." We think to ourselves, "Interesting, because you seem to love reading your text messages on the sly." The student doesn't hate reading; she hates *this* specific text. However, one difficulty gets universalized, thus debilitating positive action toward tackling a tough text.

And we do this ourselves. Ever glance at a class roster and think, "This is going to be a rough group"? I have. But I've learned to catch myself when universalizing a class. Sure, I've had groups that have a *lot* of difficult students. But lost within this univer-salization of a "troubled roster" are the many students who love learning and want to be there. As we saw in Chapter 1, when we universalize something bad, we not only focus on it more, but we also lose sight of the good, due to inattentional blindness.

Want other examples of universalizing an adversity? Spilling a coffee and thinking, "Today sucks." Having a rough lesson and saying, "I'm a bad teacher." Suffering some bad interactions with a couple of colleagues and thinking, "I can't stand this staff."

A couple of final points are helpful before coaching yourself to practical optimism. First, ask yourself, in which situations are you optimistic (specific and temporary) when responding to adversities? Then, ask yourself, in which situations are you pessimistic (universal and permanent)? Our explanatory style is contextual. You might be optimistic in your classroom when a lesson goes sour but pessimistic when the administration makes a decision you don't like. Or you may rebound quickly from a bit of strife in a relationship but simmer in a permanent, universal stew of rumination after a parent gripes. Be aware of your cognitive habits in varying contexts.

Secondly, a cognitive shift will take more than a couple of reframings. Each of us has developed our style after decades of self-talk. So we'll have to be vigilant and consistent in coaching ourselves. The effort, though, is worth it for our well-being.

Life Assignments

Now that you understand the importance of practical optimism, it's time to take action. Here are a few pathways to follow.

Assignment #1: Enlist a Language Coach

By the time we're adults, thought patterns have been habituated in our mind for decades, so we're often oblivious to them. This is where a language coach can be helpful. Task a colleague, partner, or student to tactfully give you feedback about some of your language habits. Your language coach might, for example, simply note how often she hears you say absolutes like "always" or "never" over the course of the week. Or she might prompt you to analyze your own thoughts, saying, "How can you frame that adversity in a more temporary way?"

If you don't like the idea of bringing in someone else, use a visual cue or reminder to reflect on your language. When I have rough days at school, I often prompt myself by reflecting on what's going on. I ask myself: "What adversity am I currently battling?

How can I specify the cause? What action steps do I need to take to reduce this adversity?"

Assignment #2: Dispute Yourself

One of the most common and effective ways to develop a more optimistic response to adversity is to dispute your pessimistic thoughts (Seligman, 2011). You might think it's crazy to debate with yourself, but realize this: you already do this every time you try to talk yourself down from those delicious donuts in the staff lounge.

Once you recognize that you're thinking something pessimistic, use one of these sentence stems to dispute pessimism:

For universalized beliefs:

"Just because [adversity], that doesn't mean [universal statement]. In reality, [more specific belief]."

Examples:

"Just because I have a dozen students who are out of control right now, that doesn't mean every kid is a disaster. In reality, I have a lot of great kids who are eager to learn."

"Just because I'm frustrated doesn't mean that whole lesson was a flop. In reality, it was only the assessment piece that went awry."

For permanent beliefs:

Swap absolutes with temporaries, followed by *action steps.*

Pessimistic:

"I can never transition without losing the flow of the lesson."

Optimistic revision:

"I am struggling right now to transition without losing the flow of the lesson. *I need to get feedback from a colleague.*"

Pessimistic:

"They always send me the students with behavior issues."

Optimistic revision:

"They've been sending me a lot of the students with behavior issues lately. *I need to connect with my administrator about getting more support.*"

Assignment #3: Analyze Others

Look externally to build your thought-coaching abilities. Although you're attuned to students using pessimistic language such as "I'm just not a math person," permanent and universalized language can be spotted anywhere. A lot of studies have analyzed the explanatory styles of managers, coaches, and politicians. Surprise, surprise: Optimistic responses to adversities yield statistical advantages (Rettew & Reivich, 1995; Seligman, 2011).

Considering our political climate, there's no shortage of speeches, press conferences, articles, or statements that can be analyzed. This is also a great way to weave explanatory style into the thread of the classroom. Analyze historical documents for optimistic or pessimistic language. Have students bring in quotations showing specific and temporary responses to adversities.

Assignment #4: Flip the Context

One of the nerdiest things I've ever done is join a vintage baseball team. It's pretty much exactly as it sounds: a bunch of other nerds teaming up to play baseball according to 1860s rules. No gloves. Wool uniforms. Vintage vocab. *Huzzah!* Players in the league ranged from 12-year-olds to guys pushing 80.

I learned two things playing vintage baseball: my baseball skills are atrocious, and I'm pessimistic when I lack baseball skills. Playing an unfamiliar sport showed me how much explanatory style hinges on context. I would approach the plate; swing at and miss a slow, underhand pitch from a septuagenarian; and devolve into permanent, universal rants about how unathletic I am.

One time, during a particularly horrendous performance, I was sulking hard on the sideline. Then I remember thinking, "If this were teaching instead of baseball, would I talk to myself like this?" No. In that moment, I realized the power of flipping the context.

When you find yourself in a pessimistic mode, imagine the adversity in a different context, one in which you're more optimistic. For example, if you're pessimistic with challenging students, but optimistic in your relationship with your partner and other family members. Think to yourself, "If I were having these troubles with my family, how would I think differently in order to not give up?"

Recognize the contexts in which you're optimistic and use them as a reference.

Assignment #5: Revise the Narrative

Despite our best intentions to stay positive, we'll still be confronted each day with adversities and challenges. Though these problems will affect us, we should consider to what extent our self-talk makes the issue worse.

In Buddhism, there's a great analogy about "the second dart." According to Buddha, adversities in life are like the first dart hitting us. We are human and feel pain when there is loss or injury. But often our reactions to the first dart are like a second dart we throw at ourselves. We create a narrative in our mind trying to explain why the first dart hit us—and that narrative often exacerbates the negative.

Want to see this concept in action? Watch the narrative unfold the next time the copy machine jams. A broken copier can be an injury—a first dart—to your plans. You might have to change your lesson plan or spend extra time waiting for repair. But as soon as the first dart hits, the narrative begins. You might find yourself stirring up more negative emotion by blaming others:

the mysterious teacher who left the machine jammed, the shoddy engineer who built that defunct dinosaur, the villainous legislator who stripped the school budget instead of buying functioning technology. You may even deprecate yourself, stewing about how you should have been more organized ahead of time. *Stupid, stupid, stupid me!*

These second darts are a product of the narratives we choose to make. And we aren't just seeing a different reality. Sometimes we're building a complete fiction in our minds, making assumptions and labels not grounded in truth.

We can't always avoid the first darts of life, but we can revise the narratives we tell ourselves in order to avoid the second (and fiftieth) darts. Recognize the next time you're rationalizing an issue and building a narrative in your mind. Then ask yourself, "What is a different version of this story? What else is just as likely? In what ways is this not as bad as I first thought?" Reality is subjective, so consider which version of truth will most move you forward.

Do this with student "behavior narratives" as well—the stories we generate in our mind to explain a student's actions. Just this year I had a kid who was volatile, truant, and apathetic. I had many stories about his lack of respect, his disregard for education. And then he stayed after class one day and explained to me that he had to take off days from school to look after his siblings, how his father had left their family when he was young, how his mother was on and off drugs. I was embarrassed to know how much my narrative was an absurd fiction.

Since you're creating a narrative in your mind to explain student behavior, why not form a rationale that still gives you the hope, motivation, and patience to make your interactions productive? Not only can a revised narrative fuel your motivation, but it might be closer to the truth than you think.

We deal with a lot of different "glasses" in education. Let's free ourselves of the pressure of dispositional optimism—that rosy view that everything is always great. Let's allow ourselves to be frustrated and challenged by the many adversities we battle in pursuit of helping others. But let's never resign ourselves to accepting adversities as permanent, universal ropes tying us to defeat. Our optimistic attitudes toward adversity create consequences of hope and resilience for ourselves and others. Take whatever glass you're given—no matter how leaky—and lift it higher. Cheers to living and modeling practical optimism!

Attitude: Empathy

One of the best decisions I ever made was watching the documentary film *Gleason*. One of the worst decisions I ever made was watching *Gleason* on a flight while sitting between two strangers.

Here's a summary of *Gleason*. Former New Orleans Saints football player Steve Gleason starts documenting his life shortly after being diagnosed with amyotrophic lateral sclerosis (ALS). Just a couple of weeks after the diagnosis, he finds out that his wife is pregnant with their first child. The documentary follows the Gleasons for five years as Steve records advice for his son, works to raise awareness for ALS, and tries to be a good father and husband—all while losing the ability to walk, speak, and control his body.

Though I've given you the gist, I cannot recommend highly enough that you watch the film. I also cannot recommend more highly that you don't do it surrounded by strangers because it will give you some intense feelings.

I watched it on a plane as two strangers listened to me bounce between stifled laughter and (barely) suppressed sobbing. I'd like to think there's some study out there about high altitudes exacerbating mood swings and making eyes leak more easily. But let's face it: I'm soft, especially when it comes to stories about dads and their sons.

What's incredible about the experience of watching *Gleason* on that plane—besides the fact that I did not flop onto my neighbor's shoulder in a wet, weepy mess—is the mental phenomenon that allowed me to be moved by that story. The life, the experiences, the emotions of some guy I've never met, via a screen, reached into my brain and triggered a roller coaster of thoughts and feelings. Despite not *really* knowing a single thing about what it's like to be Steve Gleason, my mind placed me into his world, allowing me to imagine the turmoil and triumph of his life.

This kind of thing happens to us every day. We cringe seeing that awkward kid spill his books across the hallway. We anticipate a student's cognitive struggle, answering the question before it's asked. We crack up on our lunch break watching triplets on YouTube giggling in unison. We even scream at our televisions when a ref makes a bad call, taking personal offense as we sit on our couches.

Our brains are capable of performing a miraculous feat that makes possible the cornerstones of civilization: marriage, friendship, education. Our brains empathize.

Empathy allowed me to make meaning out of *Gleason*, connecting with a stranger on a screen and rethinking how I approach my daily life. Empathy lets us feel our partner's frustration without that person saying a word. It helps us step back before snapping in anger, working to collaborate rather than control.

Social science is booming right now with efforts to understand empathy. Some researchers are tracing its evolutionary roots; some are looking at its limitations; and others are just trying to define what the heck it is. There are whole books and doctoral theses on empathy. This information, though, is for the practical educator who wants real strategies to reduce conflict, deepen relationships, and renew passion for teaching. We will look at two of the biggest reasons we should try to connect with others:

- Lack of connection leads to more interpersonal conflict, which diminishes our well-being.
- When we don't feel a connection with our students and colleagues, we lose sight of why we fell in love with teaching.

We should start by coming together on what empathy is.

An Unfussy Definition of Empathy

Many folks get hung up on the differences between empathy, sympathy, and compassion. Brene Brown, author, professor, and emotion researcher, has argued, as many do, that "empathy fuels connection, while sympathy drives disconnection" (2013). The gist of the "empathy is superior" argument is that empathy is sharing a similar emotion, whereas sympathy, rooted in feeling bad for someone, creates a gap between our fortune and someone else's misfortune (e.g., bummer that you're down there while I'm doing well up here).

On the flip side, we have Yale psychologist Paul Bloom, who argues that empathy creates larger-scale divides, reasoning that compassion rooted in sympathy is key (2017).

For those of you who like to philosophize, pick a camp. I, however, have too many papers to grade and lessons to plan to get caught up in pedantic semantics. I've benefited by settling on this standard: *Look for common ground of emotion and experience and use it to connect, understand, and help someone.*

At its core, empathy is our natural process of understanding others so that we can better bond and build with friends or stay away and survive foes. Empathy promotes survival by helping us navigate the complex world of human relationships.

Despite how basic empathy is and how it's wired into our brains, we should understand the components of empathy, how it affects our relationships, and what its limitations are. In doing so, we can upgrade our factory-issue empathy from a surviving mechanism to a thriving mechanism.

Three Types of Empathy

Visualize your nemesis from grade school, the kid who tormented you in various ways. This nemesis no doubt lacked empathy, unable to put himself into your shoes, right? For years, the common narrative has been that bullies lack empathy. But academics are starting to realize that this is only partially true. It turns out that there are different *types* of empathy (Goleman, 2008):

- **Cognitive empathy**—The ability to take someone else's perspective and imagine what he is thinking;
- **Affective (emotional) empathy**—The ability to feel the emotion that someone else might feel; and
- **Compassionate empathy**—The ability to feel someone else's unpleasant emotion *and* feel moved to help or support.

Your school nemesis didn't lack *each* type of empathy. In fact, your antagonist probably was capable of cognitive empathy. Aggressors are quite adept at anticipating what you might be thinking, which is why they're masterful at getting under your skin. Taking an adversary's perspective via cognitive empathy can be used for ill (such as torture or manipulation) or personal gain (such as negotiating a better deal).

Although cognitive empathy can be used for deviance, it isn't automatically bad. In fact, from a teaching standpoint, a lack of cognitive empathy can create what educational researcher John Hattie (2012) calls an empathy *gap*: being so knowledgeable about our content that we're unable to imagine what it's like for someone who doesn't understand the subject. We've all been smacked in the face by assuming that a student will grasp something easily just because it seems easy to *us*.

Don't bail on cognitive empathy just because some use it for ill purpose. We need it. We also, though, need to *feel* others' emotions and not just *think* their thoughts. We need affective empathy. Studies are somewhat mixed on the relationship between cognitive empathy and bullying. Sometimes more cognitive empathy equals more bullying; however, a more consistent finding is that more affective empathy is linked to a smaller likelihood of bullying (Van Noorden, Haselager, Cillessen, & Bukowski, 2014).

But wait. There's also a downside to sharing others' feelings too deeply. Academics call this an empathy *trap*: relating so much to another's feelings that we *don't* act compassionately. According to Stanford neurologist Robert Sapolsky, "Pain is painful.... If you're mostly focused on, 'What would this feel like if it were happening to me?' that's the predictor of people who don't necessarily make that leap from feeling empathy to actually acting compassionately" (Levy, Howard, & Aronczyk, 2018).

Imagine, for example, a crisis responder empathizing too deeply with the victim of a crime. The resulting flood of emotions such as fear and reaction to pain might render the responder incapable of detaching enough to act logically. The same is true for a social worker who carries too much of a client's trauma home with him after work. Sharing too much of another's unpleasant emotion creates avoidance, not compassionate action.

As educators, we totter above both pitfalls of empathy. Each year we get more knowledgeable about content and further from the experience of our students, widening our empathy gaps. Yet we're exposed to the depths of student strife and trauma, which can pull us into the empathy trap of bearing the weight of the world on our shoulders. To deal with empathy traps, emotion experts like Paul Ekman argue that we should cue compassionate empathy—allowing ourselves to empathize with someone's emotional state, but just enough to engage a response to help or support in some way (Goleman, 2008).

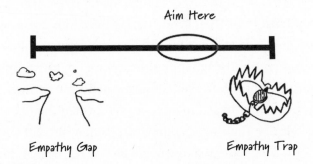

In one respect then, we shouldn't empathize so deeply that we cannot function as teachers. Be aware of empathy traps. However, my experience has shown me that a *lack* of empathy can create the larger drain on our well-being—and longevity—as educators. Therefore, let's focus more on building common ground and minimizing empathy gaps. More intentionally increasing our empathy is beneficial for many reasons.

Differences widen empathy gaps. Students are in a different place than we are: their stresses, worries, and experiences differ from ours. Although emotions and the awkwardness of adolescence may be universal, our students are growing up in a different generational context. Research finds that, although we're good at empathizing with similar experiences, we lack affective empathy when someone has a different experience than we do (Silani, Lamm, Ruff, & Singer, 2013). We need to shrink these gaps.

Bad moods impair empathy. Experimental studies find that when people are in a bad mood, the neural mechanisms necessary for empathizing are impaired (Li, Meng, Li, Yang, & Yuan, 2017; Suttie, 2017). We're also worse at mirroring others' actions and facial expressions when we're down (Kuhbandner, Pekrun,

& Maier, 2010; Likowski et al., 2011). The very moments when we should empathize more—when we're having a rough moment with a student—are the moments when empathizing is hardest. We need to be able to flip the switch and avoid downward spirals.

Empathy is good for student-teacher relationships. One controlled study out of Stanford found powerful effects when teachers went through brief empathy training. Teachers watched online instructional modules on empathy two months apart. Their students were also surveyed and behavioral records were kept. Compared to a control group (which watched online modules on technology and learning), suspension rates for the empathy group were 50 percent lower. And students who were normally suspended reported feeling more respected by their teacher—just as respected as students who weren't likely to be suspended (Okonofua, Paunesku, & Walton, 2016).

Finding connections improves academic performance. If you're already worried that this jabbering about empathy is too touchy-feely, too nonacademic (*But what about the test scores?*), ease up. A study of two dozen teachers and hundreds of students looked at the effects of social connectedness between students and teachers on student learning. After students were surveyed individually, researchers gave some teachers reports on what they had in common with some of their students without any direction on what to do with the information. However, the students with whom teachers identified common connections earned higher achievement scores. For minority students, this translated to a 60 percent reduction in the achievement gap (Gehlbach et al., 2016).

You probably don't need tomes of research to tell you the benefits of positive relationships built on common connections. The challenge, though, is making empathy an intentional strategy—especially in moments of discord or clashing with someone. We can learn about conflict reduction by thinking about a moment of literal clashing: the sinking of the *Titanic*.

What's significant for our purpose is the interaction between the ship and the iceberg. Icebergs are a great analogy for empathy because what we see in others' actions is only a fraction of the whole hunk of ice. What wrecked the *Titanic* was the collision below the surface of the water. Similarly, what wrecks our relationships and ability to connect with others is ignoring—or not considering—what is below the surface of a person's behavior.

Consider the "tip" to be the behavior we see: the decisions, the words, the nonverbal indicators. Often, we look to address or understand only what we see.

John Gottman, renowned relationship expert, says that the number-one cause of conflict in a relationship is "nothing" (2012). What we think we're arguing about—or what conflicts are present in a classroom—isn't the real issue. The conflict stems from underlying tensions and attitudes. Teachers clash with students over tardiness after lunch, the interruption when we're talking, the texting in class. But it's not *really* about the tardiness, the interruption, the texting. It's about the values and emotions that lie below the surface of these outward behaviors.

If you think about the last clash you had with someone, you can see that the visible argument—the "thing" being debated—was only the tip of the iceberg. Consider the example of an infamous dirty-dishes dispute between two people.

Person A (my wife) sees the dirty dishes piled in the sink. She sighs and starts scrubbing, muscles tensed, dishes clashing. Person B (me) observes the scene, senses he's in trouble, and tersely says, "Don't worry about those now. I'll take care of them later tonight."

Person A responds with a classic, "No, it's fine."

Person B—knowing well the true meaning of this camouflaged snake of a word, "fine"—is paralyzed with the fear that comes with countless futile efforts to overcome "fineness." So he attempts to take over the cleaning.

"Let me help."

"Stop. I've got it."

"Okaaaay, I was just trying to help."

And you know what happens next: aggressive scrubbing; monosyllabic utterings; debate and argument about standards and philosophies of dish cleaning. But we all know it wasn't *really* about the dishes. The din of dishes, the words, the irritated nonverbal indicators are just the visible behaviors. The *causes* of those behaviors are below the surface: moods, history, conflict styles.

When we look below the surface at the causes and contexts of the behavior, we're more likely to empathize. In doing so, we're less likely to get riled up, ruminate, or resent, all of which destroy our well-being.

In the dirty-dishes example, with my wife as Person A and myself as Person B, I need to pause before I respond and consider why my wife is showing these visible behaviors. For example, I can do some simple mental telepathy and realize the following factors, among many:

- My wife feels unsettled when things don't appear orderly.
- It's late at night, so she's tired.
- She had a rough day with her students.
- I've been saying "I'll take care of it later" for two days now.

Practicing a few seconds of affective empathy doesn't necessarily change her behavior, but it does change mine, which can either mitigate or exacerbate the conflict. Because I care about my wife, it catalyzes compassionate empathy, the effort to help ease someone's suffering. These moments allow me to be more patient when, for example, she rejects my first effort to help. Empathizing also allows me to be more flexible in considering what else I can do to show her I understand and care, such as drying the dishes she washed, or starting to clean other parts of the kitchen that are dirty.

The iceberg analogy encourages us to look more deeply at the sources of human behavior. From a teaching standpoint, doing so creates a proactive approach to relationships rather than a reactive approach.

Typically, when a student misbehaves, we address the action—the visible behavior—first. Even when we ask questions like "What are you doing?" we're often questioning rhetorically rather than empathetically. We know what the student is doing. We see it. The deeper question is "What triggered this behavior?"

Notice when your questions are about the visible behavior rather than the underlying causes and emotions. Then, reframe the question to explore what's below the surface:

- What is he doing? → What triggered this behavior?
- What do I need to say right now? → What do I need to know or consider before I speak?
- How do I get him to agree with me? → What about his view can I understand or agree with?
- How does he not understand X? → What does he need in order to understand X?

A shift in the question creates a shift in the power dynamics. A reactive, out-loud "What are you doing?" is an attempt at control (and we all know how power struggles work with most students).

A proactive, internal question such as "What triggered this behavior?" allows us to go deeper, to work *with* a student to understand him. As a teacher I'm not just working to suppress a behavior; I'm working to understand an emotion that is coming out sideways from a student.

Ultimately, affective and compassionate empathy are about reducing the likelihood that conflict, tension, and unpleasant emotions will spiral out of control. We have enough life evidence proving that interpersonal conflict is bad for our well-being. If we pause to look at what's below the surface, we avoid colliding with conflict and sinking our well-being.

Life Assignments

The iceberg analogy and flipping the question are two attitude shifts that can transform our actions into compassionate empathy. Here are a few more assignments for making actions and attitudes intentional.

Assignment #1:
Do a "Know-Thyself" Check

One personal epiphany is that 70 percent (non-peer-reviewed estimate) of the time, my anger at a class or a student stems from the same emotion: fear that *I* failed. When students aren't following along in a lesson, my anger is usually disappointment that I didn't plan the lesson better—it's boring, confusing, or not relevant. My frustration with a student not making progress on an essay is often rooted in my feeling incompetent at explaining the assignment well. Sometimes we need to look at our own emotional triggers, not just others'.

It took me years to realize the importance of looking at my own iceberg—knowing what root emotion was causing discontent. So I adapted a phrase that every counselor and psychiatrist knows well—the I-statement:

"I feel [emotion] because [cause]. I need/want [specific action]."

Normally, I-statements are used between two people to maturely address external conflict. However, I also use them reflectively to reduce internal conflict. For example, before I snap at my students for asking a lot of questions about the upcoming assignment, I think, "I'm impatient because, really, I didn't model this assignment well. I need to ask everyone to pause in asking questions and to watch me or hear me as I provide an example." Before I yell at a kid for texting in class, I check myself: "I feel disrespected because it seems like he doesn't value this class. I need to talk with him one-on-one to understand why he's on his phone so much and explain to him why that feels disrespectful."

A keystone of being able to relate to someone else's emotion is being able to identify our own, which is what an internal I-statement cues. I call this strategy a "know-thyself" check, and I use it whenever I feel that red-cheeked anger starting to build.

On the topic of anger, the more precise we are in labeling the emotion, the more we can see the root cause. Anger is a vague emotion, and some even consider it a response to a deeper emotion. For that reason, I try to eliminate *anger* as a label. I also try to cut these vague descriptors: *upset, irritated, emotional* (we always have emotion, so we're always emotional).

Sometimes a know-thyself check is just an internal reset to help us understand ourselves. Often it leads to more proactive and collaborative conflict reduction.

Assignment #2: Use the 4-L Process

Nursing scholar Teresa Wiseman realized that patients who feel empathy from their caregivers also feel more positive about their medical care. After years of studying the existing research and theories on empathy, Wiseman identified four defining attributes of empathy:

1. Perspective taking (seeing the world as others see it)
2. Being nonjudgmental
3. Understanding another's feelings
4. Communicating the understanding of his/her emotions (Wiseman, 1996)

Because I'm a teacher, and therefore obsessed with mnemonics, I've adjusted these attributes into a process I call the 4-L Process:

1. *Label* the emotion you think the person is feeling.
2. *Link* this moment to a time when you've felt a similar emotion (or reacted in a similar way).
3. *Listen* nonjudgmentally; ask the person to talk about what she is experiencing.
4. *Let go* of any resentment you're holding and remember that this person is human.

Depending on the context, it might also be helpful to *let* the person know that you identify with an emotion he or she is feeling.

You can use the 4 (or 5) *L*s for more than just mitigating conflict. Use the process to empathize in moments when you normally get grumpy—at staff meetings, for instance. When a colleague goes on a tangent about the dress code, I try to run through the process, which goes something like this:

1. *Label:* She might feel isolated because she senses that she's the only one upholding the handbook rules.
2. *Link:* I've felt similar isolation when I hold kids accountable for tardiness and they gripe, "Other teachers don't make a huge deal about this!"
3. *Listen:* I should probably at least listen to her thoughts before I judge.
4. *Let go:* Sure, I'd like to go home now; but in the grand scheme, this two-minute tirade won't ruin my day.

A bonus to using the 4-L process is that, once we memorize the steps, we can cue them when we start to get worked up. When our unpleasant emotions try to hijack our thinking, we can automatically switch on logic and compassionate empathy.

Assignment #3: Get the Backstory

We read the news and see tragedies all over the world. Yet we often aren't moved to take much action. Journalists are even experimenting with "anthropographics," using human-looking images to represent statistics, as a way to elicit empathy. Unfortunately, even a stat dressed as a real human doesn't influence us much (Bertini, 2017). For the unknown sufferer, psychologists recommend practices called "Put a Human Face on Suffering" (Greater Good in Action, n.d.). These usually involve zeroing in on a specific person's narrative and empathizing with that person's circumstances—or even meditating to feel compassion toward the sufferer.

As educators, we sometimes have the opposite problem: we have the face of a student in front of us every day, but we don't know the narrative. Yet we've also experienced the powerful shift that comes with hearing a student's backstory.

A few years ago, I was shocked when a student flipped out in the middle of a lesson, shoving his books to the ground, yelling "[Expletive] this!" and storming out the room. No one had even said anything to him to provoke the outburst. He simply snapped.

Then I learned some of the backstory. I pulled him into my room during lunch, asked him what happened, and listened. Within seconds he started bawling—an alpha male, muscle-jacked football player choked with tears. He released a flood of his anxieties: how no one in his family went to college and his grades suck and his only hope is a football scholarship and he is ineligible because of his grades in my class. How he puts on a front to act like he doesn't care—but he does and he feels dumb. How every day he hears racial slurs in the hallway as he battles two identities: being targeted as one of the few students of color in school and being taunted by his cousins for "acting white."

For the first time, I had a glimpse of the backstory, the stuff below the surface. I knew that his outburst in my class wasn't about me or the lesson. I was embarrassed that I had thought of myself as the victim in the scenario—the do-gooder teacher disrespected by the student. I couldn't come close to having experienced what that kid had, but I could empathize with some of the emotions, even if only with a sliver of their intensity. And even the feeling that *I couldn't* fully empathize with his experience was powerful: it told me I had to work harder to try to understand his world before taking offense that he didn't understand mine.

Behind every action, there is a backstory. Learn the narrative.

Although we might not have a chance to sit down with every student the way I did with that student, we can always find a way to dig deeper into the iceberg and get some backstory. Here are some ways to do this.

Life check. Once a month, give students 5 or 10 minutes to write in response to this prompt: *What's going on in your world that would be helpful for me to know?* I let students know that their writing is a safe space, that I will keep it confidential (unless, of course, it falls into the realm of what I'm mandated to report and get them support for). And I respond, letting them know that I've read what they wrote and that I empathize with them.

Consult the tribe. My first go-to when I don't understand a student's behavior is to consult someone else who understands the student better. Counselors, former teachers, coaches, and parents are all great sources to learn more about a student's history. I've even asked friends of a student. A simple question to ask is this: "What would be helpful to know about this student's background in order to better teach him?" Here's a rule of thumb: get one piece of evidence about a student's backstory for every assumption you have about the student's outward behavior.

Resilience stories. When thinking about backstory, we often frame our attention around trauma that negatively affects a student. Reframe the focus and ask students to consider moments in which they were resilient in handling something that happened in their lives. Have them write a summary of a moment when they overcame something difficult—what it was, what they learned, and how the experience may empower them in the future.

Provide similar prompts or stems to have students consider moments they felt pride or a sense of accomplishment. These stories will help you not only understand their world but also see their strengths.

Scale of 1–10 (or "thumb-ometer"). Before getting into content, I often ask students to check in with their nearby peers about how their day is going so far. These 30-second chats are good opportunities for them to learn more about one another. I also follow up by having them quickly show on their hands, via a scale of 1 to 10, how they are doing. I don't have them elaborate, but I do make a mental note of which students are lower on the scale (especially if this seems consistent). I make a note to monitor those students, to be patient if they aren't on their A-game, and to have a one-on-one chat if time allows. The 1–10 scale can be modified to a "thumb-ometer," with students noting their mood by positioning their thumb down, up, or somewhere in between.

Assignment #4: Conduct Common Ground Surveys

As cited earlier, when teachers and students identify common connections with one another, this can translate to not only better relationships but also better academic performance (Gehlbach et al., 2016). We often give students surveys asking them about their interests and hobbies. But we can build connection by more actively helping them find connections with us.

Share your own survey results in which you list your favorites—foods, music, hobbies, interests, video-streaming binges.

Then have students respond to a simple prompt: *Based on what you know about me, what do we have in common?* Students can even fill in a simple matching-response sheet to note similarities (see the example in Appendix B: Making Connections with a Common Ground Survey). Consider doing this activity with staff and administration as well.

Eighteen-plus years as a student and a decade as a teacher have shown me one truth: human connection is the keystone of education and of living a good life.

The drive to learn is stifled when we feel disconnected. The drive to teach is suffocated when we lose sight of our influence on others and our commonality as people.

Students enter our classrooms every day, and we get to *choose* whether to relate to them. Consider though, that our lives are colliding with theirs whether we choose to connect. Our choice to empathize can shift this moment from a cataclysm of negative friction to a catalyst of positive action. We can work—and feel—*with* rather than beside or against.

I may regret having chosen to watch an intense movie on an airplane, but I have never regretted the choice to find common ground with the people who enter my classroom or my life.

7

Attitude: Forgiveness

Holding a grudge is like drinking poison
and waiting for the other person to die.

—Unknown

I thought Godzilla was ripping off our rain gutter in a two-second rage. The shrill slice and grind of crunching metal startled me, my wife, and our paranoid dog. I bolted to our window and saw our neighbor, who shared the driveway, stepping from his car to look at the damage he had done. Not knowing I had a creeper's eye on him, he looked around, picked up the gutter he'd smashed with his car, and shoved it back onto our lawn before peeling off.

I was annoyed. My wife was apoplectic. She fumed about how disrespectful our neighbor was, how I needed to confront him, how he better fix it. I can't blame my wife for getting fired up because our gutter was ruined—and she was in labor.

Hours later she gave birth to our son and the whole gutter matter drifted out of memory. I had a newborn to love.

I forgot about the gutter until we drove home from the hospital and I saw the mangled metal crumpled on our lawn. Although I had more important things to worry about, my anger started building. I hoped my neighbor would have done the right thing and fixed it, but he hadn't.

Weeks later, this neighbor and I sat outside talking, a few feet away from "the evidence." I waited for him to say he was sorry, to offer to fix the damage. He walked away without a word. Now *I* was ready to rupture. I ran through scenario after scenario—what I should have said, what I *needed* to say, what revenge I should take— to make him cower in remorsefulness and repair the damage.

Eventually, I repaired it myself. Months later, though, I was still fuming every time I saw that gutter. I *resented* my neighbor.

Resentment and the Harm It Causes

Resentment. You've experienced it—possibly within the last 24 hours. Resentment is the ruminating anger we hold when how a person acts doesn't fit our conception of how we want that person to act.

How a Person Acts   How I Want a Person to Act

For me, I expected my neighbor to own his mistake when he damaged my property. But he didn't. Ever. And so I spun the web of anger in my mind again and again until my entire view of him changed.

As educators, we also resent. Our job involves a challenging balance between having high expectations for our students and working with . . . kids, who are still very much "in process."

In other words, our days are filled with students behaving in ways that don't match our high expectations. If this mismatch happens intensely or often enough, the disappointment turns to resentment, circulating in our minds and consuming thoughts that could be used for far more productive things.

Which student have you resented? Which colleague? Which parent? I can name a handful. Even as I write this, their faces and words get kicked up out of subconscious dust and threaten to pollute my happiness. I'm willing to bet you even have names that, when you hear them, trigger animosity.

The true detriment of resentment is this: the person experiencing the emotional anguish is the resenter, not the resentee. At most, a student is thrilled that she got under my skin. At bare minimum, the student doesn't even care (or know). In either case, I'm the one steeping in psychological acid.

We're not just talking in abstractions. An inability to let go of resentment can wreak havoc on our mental and physical health. For example, not only does resentment toward a past wrong increase negative emotions like anger, but it can also affect our biochemistry, making our cortisol spike and increasing the strain on our cardiovascular system (Witvliet, Ludwig, & Vander Laan, 2001).

Resentment casts darkness across our whole world. Consider how deeply resentment affects our past, present, and future:

- My past: My memories associated with the event or person are tainted by a focus on the negatives.
- My present: Even as I think about my past or interact with that person in the present, I feel unpleasant emotions; I ruminate.
- My future: I develop a pessimism for future interactions with this person or situation, which may lead to the following:
  - Deepening my bias

- Learned helplessness
- Self-fulfilling prophecies (predictive encoding) of bad experiences

Response to Offense

Let's explore the germination of rumination. Imagine some-one did something that affected you negatively. Maybe a student was disrespectful during a lesson, or a colleague said something negative about you to a coworker. Perhaps a parent implied that you're a glorified babysitter. What happens when you revisit this moment?

First, I hope, you went through a process of problem solving and addressed the situation maturely. But even if you *did* deal with the situation to prevent it from happening again, thinking about the offense may stir up resentment. We see that student, that col-league, that parent again and the cantankerous memories crawl out of our brain. What do we do? Most likely, we'll take one of three paths:

1. Ruminate.
2. Suppress the emotion. (Think about the moment but try not to let any negative emotions emerge.)
3. Reappraise our feelings about the experience, the offender, or both.

In Chapter 2 we examined why rumination, the first option, erodes our well-being. Not only does rumination abrade our happiness, but, contrary to what we may think, it makes us *less* competent at resolving interpersonal conflict (Lyubomirsky & Nolen-Hoeksema, 1995). Letting ourselves ruminate about the offense may intensify negative emotions and dampen positive emotions. If we ruminate enough, we wire a deep-seated anger about a person into our brain. *Rumination is a fuel on the resent-ment fire.*

What about the second option, suppressing the emotion? We might think, "As long as I don't *act* out on my resentment, there's no problem. I can plot the downfall of my administrator, but as long as I don't *do* anything, it's all good, right?" Unfortunately, that's not the case. In the short term, we may reduce the negative emotions a bit, but suppressing emotions isn't a good long-term solution.

Studies have found that suppressing negative emotions has adverse physical and emotional health effects, such as increasing our sympathetic nervous system (fight-or-flight response), increasing our blood pressure, decreasing positive emotion, depleting cognitive resources, and reducing social support (Witvliet, DeYoung, Hofelich, & DeYoung, 2011). Not ideal.

In other words, trying to simply suppress resentment is like having a stone stuck in our shoe that we try to shake to the side. We may ignore it for a little while, but it creeps back under our foot until we take the shoe off and dump the stone. In much the same way, at some point we need to stop, address the resentment, and let go of our ruminating mental anguish. Revenge may sound sweet, but research shows that it increases rumination, decreases happiness, and fails to decrease negative affect (Carlsmith, Wilson, & Gilbert, 2008; Watson, Rapee, & Todorov, 2015).

Ending resentment has less to do with the other person's behavior and more to do with our choice, our view, our mental framing. And the most powerful choice we can make to end resentment is this: *forgive.*

Forgiveness is the process of reappraising our feelings toward a transgression or transgressor to minimize resentment. Forgiving is a mental choice (or series of choices) to recognize that we cannot control others' behaviors or change the past—but we can change our thoughts, our actions, and our motives to move forward.

Although forgiveness is the solution to ending resentment, it's hard to undertake. So if we're going to take on the daunting decision to forgive, we should probably know what's in it for us.

Benefits of Forgiveness

Let's talk about that heart you have for teaching—not the symbolic "Oooh, I love people" heart, but the muscle that feeds oxygen to your brain. If you're in the habit of holding resentment, you're damaging that critical organ.

Compared to ruminating about an offense, visualizing forgiveness reduces blood pressure and heart rate and minimizes activation of the sympathetic nervous system (Witvliet et al., 2001; Witvliet et al., 2008). Even temporarily *thinking* about forgiving someone creates measurable reductions in the body's physiological stress response.

If keeping your ticker ticking isn't enough, think about other benefits that will help you thrive as a teacher (and a human). Forgiveness boosts self-esteem, increases hope, lowers anxiety, reduces depression, and minimizes anger (McCullough & Witvliet, 2001). Practicing forgiveness can even yield increased optimism and positive stress reduction up to six months after interventions (Harris et al., 2006).

It's hard to argue that forgiveness *isn't* an incredible practice for increasing our well-being. So why don't we forgive more often? It's not that we don't know the value of forgiveness, but usually we prefer being the forgiven instead of the forgiver. Forgiving others can be a difficult, stressful process (Watson et al., 2015).

We may resist forgiving because we think that, by doing so, we give up our power. Actually, the opposite is true. *When we forgive, we empower ourselves.* We choose to stop letting the past control our actions, dictate our happiness, or define our relationships.

OK, hurray for forgiveness. But if I forgive that crotchety colleague who focuses on the lemons and not the lemonade, am I condoning negativity? Must I look weak by offering reconciliation? Not at all. Let's look at some "forgiveness myths" to address these concerns.

Forgiveness Myths

Here are some of the common misconceptions about forgiveness and the corresponding truths.

Myth #1: Forgiving requires reconciliation.
Truth: We don't need to say a word to the offender to practice forgiveness.

If you're worried about the discomfort of bowing to that classroom bully, relax. Forgiveness is an internal process. Many scholars share a core component in their definitions of forgiveness: when people forgive, their thinking changes toward an offense to decrease negative feelings and increase prosocial thoughts (McCullough & Witvliet, 2001). Notice how the central focus is changing our *thinking*, regardless of whether or not we choose to reconcile.

Myth #2: Forgiving means condoning or accepting a repeated wrong.
Truth: Forgiveness often leads us to *address* a transgression with a level head instead of ignoring or accepting it.

Holding resentment prevents us from positive action because we soak in the psychological acid of negative rumination. By contrast, forgiveness is a decision to end resentment and give ourselves mental clarity and emotional resilience. It allows us to step beyond our past pain and find new direction for moving forward.

Moving forward may mean getting away from a negative environment entirely (such as an abusive situation), addressing the behavior with action steps (such as coaching student behavior), or focusing our energy on the future rather than the past (such as the day after a student meltdown). In other words, forgiveness is *not* the absence of action. It is reframing our mental state to empower ourselves to take positive action.

Myth #3: Forgive and forget, right?

Truth: "Forgive and forget" is a misstatement.

We can't force our brains to forget an unpleasant memory (believe me, I've tried to forget plenty of student terrors, to no avail). Forgiveness, then, does not mean we try to forget an injury that has affected us. And people often struggle to begin the forgiveness process because they worry that forgiveness means forgetting (Cohen, 2004).

Forgiveness maintains memory that an offense happened; however, instead of ruminating, we reappraise the memory to learn and use mental resources for more constructive action. When I forgive, I don't forget that a student lied to me about that act of plagiarism, but I do reframe that memory to humanize the student, to not hold a useless grudge, and to come from a place of coaching rather than condemning.

Myth #4: Forgiving eschews justice.

Truth: Forgiveness and justice can work together.

Say a student insults a peer. There should be a consequence, right? But if I forgive the student in my mind, am I shirking justice? No. Consider these two interesting observations about justice and forgiveness:

- Forgiveness and justice are both prosocial concepts that help society. To see the powerful combination of justice *with* forgiveness, look at the Truth and Reconciliation Commission that emerged out of the apartheid in South Africa.
- The more we believe justice has been served (or the more we are primed with the thought of justice), the more likely we are to forgive (Karremans & Van Lange, 2005).

Forgiveness can follow justice. If a consequence, a correction, or a conference is needed to ensure justice, make it happen.

But when it does happen, choose to move forward by choosing to forgive.

Life Assignments

If you're ready to stop stewing in the social-emotional acrimony of resentment, give yourself the gift of inner peace with forgiveness. Start small, with the minor offenses. It would be silly for a new runner to run a marathon as a first race, so don't start your forgiveness efforts with the big, deeply wounding offenses. Begin with the minor transgressions that keep you from being the educator you want to be. Here are some assignments to get you started.

Assignment #1:
Conduct a Resentment Burial

Turn the abstract, mental ruminations of resentment into tangible recordings that you can literally let go of. You've already replayed the mental scene of the offense (probably dozens of times). Give that scene a proper burial.

Start by writing out your description of what happened. However, don't describe the "facts" of what happened. Pinpoint how the events made you feel. Describe *why* you were affected.

A resentment burial is more than your typical venting session in the teacher lounge. After describing the offense and its effect on you, write down what you need to do to move forward, why you're choosing to forgive, and how you're a better person now that you've persevered through the transgression. Consider using these sentence stems:

- I'm moving on because _____.
- I'll move forward by _____.
- I realize now that _____.
- I forgive [transgressor or transgression] because _____.
- I'm a better person now because _____.
- In the future I will _____.

Once you've written out your thoughts fully and honestly, do something with the document. Burn it. Throw it away. Put it in a drawer to look at again the next time you're stewing. Give it a place *other* than spinning inside your mind.

Assignment #2: Rerecord the Tape

When we ruminate about an interpersonal offense, we often fill gaps in our memory or knowledge with fictional thoughts. For example, when I picture my neighbor smashing our gutter, I picture him thinking, "Whatever. Who cares about their stupid gutter. They aren't going to say anything. Forget them!"

In truth, I have no idea what was running through his mind. He could have been embarrassed by his crappy driving, rushing due to an emergency, planning on fixing the gutter soon—he could have been thinking anything. And yet, I make up the worst-case scenario. This fictionalization is my choice.

Every time we recall a memory, it has the potential to change (Bridge & Voss, 2014). Memories are not always reality. They are our malleable "historical fictions." We can choose, then, to reappraise the memory and find inner peace.

One way to do this is a process called "compassionate reappraisal." In this mental replay, we consider how the other human is, well, human—flawed, capable of mistakes, and made up of the same universal emotions we are.

When we compassionately reappraise, we imagine the memory from the other person's viewpoint, visualizing how that individual makes mistakes and does not wish us ill will. In this act of empathy and understanding, we also wish for the person to learn, to heal, and to grow so that he doesn't hurt others in the future. We consider ourselves giving a gift of mercy even if we know the relationship can't be fully repaired. This all may sound wishy-washy and weak; however, research shows that, compared to ruminating or suppressing emotion, compassionate reappraisal increases positive emotion, decreases negative emotion, and positively affects our physiology (Witvliet et al., 2011).

Also consider not making this one transgression a universal image of the entire person. In Chapter 5 we discussed the dangers of making an adversity a pervasive deal in our mind. For example, we shouldn't view a student as a completely inconsiderate person because of one inconsiderate act. If we want to be resilient, we have to see a transgression as a specific, even temporary event. Our compassionate reappraisal might include remembering moments when the person didn't wrong us or showed signs of goodness. If we're going to replay a transgression in our minds—and if it's already an *interpretation* of reality—we might as well choose a version that most accurately reflects a truth about life: people are imperfect.

Assignment #3: Establish a "Reset Ritual"

Let's be honest. Resentment and lack of forgiveness affect us teachers most when it comes to *that* student. You know the one. He enters the class each day and we get this sinking feeling of dread. We project our resentment into the future, thinking, "I *know* [insert demonized child's name here] is going to [insert horrible offense]." Each interaction we have is tainted with resentment as our nonverbal reactions leak and our stress rises.

How about a "reset ritual"? I used this during my most horrendous year of teaching *every single day*. I had a whole crew of students who made my blood pressure rise as they walked into my room. They made many mistakes that required many consequences and coaching sessions. Forgiving them was a daily affair.

So I created a ritual. Every day, before they walked in, I sat on my stool and took a slow, mindful breath. I looked at the sign strategically posted across my room that reads, "I don't quit." I reminded myself that forgiveness is the first step in resilience.

And then I would smile—even if it was a "fake it 'til you make it" grin—before saying "good morning" to the class.

Those resets were critical in reducing my resentment and rallying my resilience. Consider your own reset for *that* kid who needs it. Use a quote, a cue, a physical object—anything that will help you remember to curtail resentment. That kid might not give you the effort you want, but you can still choose to give the effort he needs.

Assignment #4: Forgive Yourself

A week before writing this chapter, CNN contacted me about coming on to discuss an article I wrote for the website We Are Teachers. It was my chance to check off a bucket-list item I never thought would *actually* happen: be on a national talk show.

The experience was terrifying. Though my performance wasn't embarrassing at the viral-video level, I didn't do as well as I wanted. If you had watched the segment, you probably wouldn't have realized my brain was aflame with anxiety. But if you know me, you would realize that I was frazzled.

As a teacher, I'm used to beating myself up about mistakes, critiquing errors, and ruminating about lessons gone wrong. But my TV experience brought on a whole new level of intra-resentment—a ruminating, self-directed anger. I was furious at myself for getting flustered and not being clear with what I wanted to say. For days I couldn't sleep because the mental movie reel was rolling with scenes of what I *should* have done better.

When is the last time you held some intra-resentment? Maybe you think back to that student you thought you could have reached, to that comment you wish you hadn't said, to that lesson that was a disaster.

The benefits of forgiveness are felt most deeply with important relationships (McCullough & Witvliet, 2001), so why not focus on the one relationship guaranteed for life: your relationship with yourself.

Self-forgiveness has major benefits, such as improving relationship satisfaction and increasing forgiveness toward others (Pelucchi, Paleari, Regalia, & Fincham, 2015).

You can approach self-forgiveness the way you would approach forgiveness toward others, such as by using the resentment-burial strategy. However, psychologist and author Rick Hanson adds that we should consider what caused our discontent: "Sort what happened into three piles: moral faults, unskillfulness, and everything else. Moral faults deserve proportionate guilt, remorse, or shame, but unskillfulness calls for correction, no more" (2015).

This act alone, of recognizing what was simply a lack of skillfulness or the result of other factors, can alleviate some of our self-directed anger. My mismanaging a difficult class, for example, isn't because I lack grace or patience; it usually is a result of lack of skill. I need to learn more strategies. Just as I wouldn't hold a grudge because a student lacks a skill such as writing thesis statements, I shouldn't hold a grudge against myself for needing more knowledge.

I lost a lot of mental space to that CNN interview in which I didn't meet my standards. I was reminded, yet again, of the importance of self-forgiveness. If forgiving others seems to be too much to take on right now, at least forgive yourself.

Assignment #5: Apologize

We've focused on how to forgive others. But what about giving others the chance to forgive us?

We've all experienced the weak, ineffectual pseudo-apology verbalized as "Sorry." Think about how you've felt when someone said, "Sorry." Perhaps it was a student who cheated on a test or threw a rock through a window. What did you feel was missing? What did you need to hear so the relationship could move forward? My guess is you wanted four things:

- Acknowledgment of the offense and why it was wrong
- An apology
- A plan for how and why it won't happen again
- Follow-through on the plan

Let's take these four "needs" and address them with a process I learned from the Quantum Learning Network, the 4-Part Apology (known as AAMR, for the first letter of the first word of each step):

1. *Acknowledge* **the offense.** Identify what you did wrong and why you think it may have affected the other person. This step establishes empathy: you demonstrate that you understand why your behavior hurt the other person.

2. *Apologize* **for negatively affecting the other person.** Because the word *sorry* is misused and abused so often, consider using the word *apologize*.

3. *Make it right* **by establishing an action plan.** Ideally, this is best done through a question, such as "What can I do to make this right?" If the person you're apologizing to doesn't know or says "Nothing," be ready with your own thoughts on how you plan to make it better.

4. *Recommit* **by following through.** Apologies are not words. Apologies are actions. If you seek forgiveness and repair, you need to change your behavior.

Here are a few tips:

- Don't foul the apology with "but" or an excuse. Own the mistake and show through your actions that you want to grow and advance.
- Use this same apology process to forgive yourself and move forward.
- If you're using this process just to get someone to reciprocate with an apology or to get out of a consequence, that's called manipulation. Don't be that person.

I lost a lot when my neighbor damaged my gutter. Not money—it cost me zero dollars (and 10 seconds) to bend the gutter back to function again. But my resentment of my neighbor cost me a lot of mental resources—resources that I didn't have to spare as I transitioned into being a new father.

I reminisce about how much mental fortitude I lost by not forgiving and letting go of pointless resentment. How much have I also lost by harboring negative thoughts about minor offenses in my classroom and in my school building?

How much have you lost as an educator when you've held grudges? How much of your health and mental resources are you *willing* to diminish by choosing to hold resentment? Make a choice to forgive transgressions. Give grace to yourself and others so that you can gain the inner peace you deserve.

Action: Altruism

The smallest act of kindness is
worth more than the grandest intention.

—Oscar Wilde

I've seen my fair share of crying teenagers. Breakups. Family challenges. A minus sign following an *A* on a paper. But a crying student on a high school field trip is rare, which is why I froze when two of my students approached me on a field trip a few years back, their eyes streaming with tears.

Their tears were ironic given that we were on our annual "altruism trip." It's a day filled with community service at a local homeless shelter, followed by planned acts of kindness for strangers in Kalamazoo, Michigan. A trip of positivity shouldn't result in tears, right?

"What's wrong?" I asked.

The students, mouths agape, were unsure how to start. Before my mind jumped to crisis-solution mode, they finally told me what had happened.

This group of students had written notes with simple compliments or positive statements to hand to people they met around town. They expressed basic sentiments, like, "Have a good day" or "You're beautiful." Students usually handed the notes out randomly. But these students had seen a woman at the city library who looked like she was having a rough day. So they picked out a specific note for her: "It will get better."

After handing the note to the lady, they walked away but then looked back to see her reaction. She read it, stood in silence among the rows of books, and started bawling. A short time later, she tracked down my students and told them that she had suffered a miscarriage a few weeks earlier.

She remarked how nothing in her world seemed to make sense after she lost her baby. But that note, "It will get better," was what she needed to have faith again. She said she saw this moment as God's way of helping her heal and find hope.

The woman and the students exchanged hugs and tears. Their exchange lasted just a few minutes, yet they, the lady at the library, and I will likely remember it forever.

One note or e-mail message can help us find hope amidst chaos. One decision to do good can make us buoyant for weeks, giving us energy and purpose. One small act of kindness can germinate across people and time and affect dozens of lives. *Kindness transcends its initial effect.*

Deciding to perform an altruistic act is one of the most empowering decisions we can make as humans—one of the most important steps to build bonds, communities, and culture. And it is one of the simplest, cheapest, and most influential actions that can improve others' lives as well as our own.

Sure, we educators are naturally altruistic folk. We pour tremendous energy into our jobs to help others, often without any tangible return (unless you get that rare kid who rewards you with the random compliment of "You aren't completely terrible").

In this chapter, we're going to expand our understanding of altruistic acts, thinking beyond the day-to-day service we give to our students and seeing the immense effect of simple, intentional acts of kindness. We'll see the benefits of kindness, its ripple effects, and the easy ways we can do more to spread positive emotion.

OK, we should probably start by addressing the elephant in the room: Isn't being kind in order to boost our well-being a selfish, contradictory act? But rather than the elephant in the room, let's address the vampire bat in the room.

Are Humans Selfish?

When you think of the *opposite* of altruism—selfishness—many images may come to mind. Violence. Thievery. Darwinian demonstrations of "survival of the fittest." But consider one of the strongest symbols we have of selfishness: the vampire bat—the beast that causes physical damage to another's well-being. Presenting bats as a paragon of self-gain creates an interesting paradox: vampire bats are both selfish *and* altruistic creatures.

On one hand, they suck blood out of other creatures. On the other hand, bats sacrifice for each other (Lehrer, 2012). Vampire bats must feed every 60 hours or they will starve to death. Not finding prey a few nights in a row can incite doom. But due to altruistic instincts, baby Dracula's buddies have his back.

If a vampire bat is starving, it will lick or touch another as a cue for help. The second bat will then regurgitate its food—sacrifice its well-being—to help. This is a gross image of altruism, I know, but it flips our assumptions of animal nature. Humans behave in the same way. No matter how much we believe that humans are inherently selfish, our lives are filled with evidence of altruistic acts.

The reality is that we *are* born with the drive to put our needs first, but we are *also* born with the drive to help others. Now, one may go on a crotchety tangent about whether *true* altruism exists. Aren't we always doing something good in the hopes that it will pay off? Isn't that inherently selfish? Isn't this chapter promoting altruism for the sake of self-gain (well-being)?

When my students bring up this question of "true altruism," I tell them this: Do an altruistic act as selflessly as possible—without expecting any return favor—and the world benefits.

When we're in a funk, want some joy, or want to feel like life has purpose, there are far worse things we could do than make someone's day better. We might not be able to fully detach our subconscious efforts for personal gain, but that shouldn't stop us from trying to be more altruistic. It's important, though, to understand what research tells us about the benefits of kindness.

Benefits of Kindness

We really shouldn't *need* a reason to be kind to others. But a little research-based nudge won't hurt. Here are just a few of the many benefits of being intentionally kind.

Short-Term Boosts

You're probably familiar with the term "helper's high," the rush of good feeling that volunteering sparks. Studies have shown a neurochemical basis for this concept. Doing good—even when just writing a check to a charity—engages the brain's "reward circuit" (Harbaugh, Mayr, & Burghart, 2007).

Resilience Boosts

We often self-indulge on stressful days, treating ourselves to retail therapy or globs of peanut butter from the jar. However, engaging in prosocial behavior increases our well-being compared to self-focused behavior, which might not have any effect on increasing positive emotion or decreasing negative emotion (Nelson-Coffey, Layous, Cole, & Lyubomirsky, 2016). Similarly, doing prosocial acts reduces the negative effects of stress, making a rough day feel less intense (Raposa, Laws, & Ansell, 2015).

Brain Boosts

Helping others is associated with better mental health (Schwartz, Meisenhelder, Ma, & Reed, 2003). Volunteering and other kind acts provide social and psychological resources that counter negative affect such as depression and anxiety, especially for the elderly (Musick & Wilson, 2003). Acts of kindness also boost life satisfaction (Buchanan & Bardi, 2010).

Seeing someone benefit from our actions makes us feel good. But even if we don't come face-to-face with the beneficiary, prosocial behavior can boost our positive affect, meaningfulness, and vitality (Martela & Ryan, 2016).

Body Boosts

The benefits of prosocial behavior go beyond psychological gains and apply to more than just older folks. A comparative study found that kids who volunteer to help others one hour a week for 10 weeks had lower cholesterol levels and lower risk factors for cardiovascular disease compared to a control group (Zakrezewski, 2013).

Another study randomly assigned 159 people to four different groups for four weeks (prosocial to specific others, prosocial to the world, kindness toward self, control). The study showed that doing kind acts improves the body's ability to fight infection or disease, as measured by leukocyte expression (Nelson-Coffey, Fritz, Lyubomirsky, & Cole, 2017). Doing good literally changes our blood.

Happy People Helping More

When we recall positive memories, we're more likely to do good for others. When researchers primed participants to think of positive experiences they had had when helping, they were more likely to help again in the future (Layous, Nelson, Kurtz, & Lyubomirsky, 2016).

Consider that intentionally choosing to do something kind, even when we're feeling crummy, might kick-start a positive-feedback loop. Doing something kind may give us more good memories to draw upon, which may trigger more kind acts (and so on). If your well-being is on the wrong track, jump the rails and get onto a track of kindness.

Not coincidentally, *receiving* an act of kindness might kick us onto an altruistic feedback loop. Depressed students who received help in getting over their suicidal thoughts are likely to help others in the same way (Greidanus & Everall, 2010). Our decision to do something kind not only makes us more likely to be prosocial in the future, it may encourage others to do the same.

The power of that idea—that acts of kindness can cascade internally and externally—cannot be overstated. One of the more remarkable findings in social psychology is the ripple effect of our decisions on those around us. As educators, we're in a prime position to infect dozens and hundreds of students with altruism because, like many behaviors, kindness is contagious.

Ripple Effects

Every educator is familiar with contagion. We see the germs swoop in and smite swaths of students as they infest our halls. Germs and diseases are contagious, as are book and music interests. But what about ideas related to obesity, divorce, or sleep hygiene?

In 2002, a group of social scientists stumbled upon a treasure trove of data: the Framingham Heart Study. Starting in 1948, the study, designed to track risk factors for heart disease, compiled a wealth of information. More than 12,000 people were surveyed about their mental health, physical health, interests, and just about anything else a researcher would want to know about a person's actions and behavior. Researchers were able to analyze "social contagion"—how ideas and behaviors spread across social networks.

This data set, along with other records of tens of thousands of people, finds that our behavior has "three degrees" of influence. Even ideas about things like obesity, divorce, and sleep hygiene often affect others who are three degrees from us (Christakis & Fowler, 2011). And—you guessed it—according to this mega-set of data, prosocial behavior is contagious. Think about that potential.

Doing something kind for a colleague doesn't just increase his likelihood of paying it forward. Being kind to Kathy can make her kinder to Alicia, who may then be kinder to Saul.

This kindness contagion effect has been found in controlled experimental studies as well. When individuals do kind, cooperative acts in simulated games, their actions are repeated by others three times over, even by those who benefited indirectly (Fowler & Christakis, 2010). In other words, *kindness leads to kindness, which leads to kindness, which leads to more kindness.*

I saw this kindness contagion firsthand when, on another altruism trip, one of my students bought coffee for a stranger behind her. More than an hour later, another group of students went to the same coffee shop, finding that the "pay it forward" act was still happening. According to the barista, over a dozen people had paid for the next stranger's drink.

Seeing kindness contagion can provide us with a sense of meaning, knowing that we caused a ripple effect of good. One altruistic act helps us feel proficient at creating positive change. It helps us build connections with others. And it provides evidence that our actions are within our control and can be used for good. No wonder, then, that kind acts engage three of our most important psychological needs: competence, relatedness, and autonomy (Martela & Ryan, 2016).

If you've felt your passion for teaching waning, remember that few, if any, professions match education for creating contagious ripple effects. We get countless opportunities to be kind to dozens of students (and colleagues), multiple times a day. We can make tidal waves of contagious compassion. But our ability to start that wave begins with how we frame the work we do.

How to Be Selfish So You Can Be Selfless

Wary of the whole eternal selflessness thing? Then know this: I support moments of selfishness.

One of the reasons teachers burn out is because sometimes we're *too selfless* and never take care of ourselves. The caveat, though, is choosing self-focused opportunities that still make us better people. Consider the following: *Am I doing* X *because the world owes me a selfish moment? Or am I doing* X *to get back to being my best so I can give my best to others?*

Here's an example. My inner introvert often screams (or whispers) for time away from others. Unfortunately, my brain gravitates toward guilt. Most often, the guilt emerges when I'm doing something lazy or wasteful under the guise of "I'm getting what I need." It's as if my brain subconsciously knows that my selfish activities—mindlessly scrolling through social media, wandering the hallways with no purpose, or binge-watching trashy TV shows—aren't going to help me get what I need.

I've learned to recognize when I'm self-focused in a way that isn't helping me be my best self. Now (usually) when I need a moment to myself, I reframe the situation with this question: *What can I do to take care of myself so that I can be a better person for others?*

Exercise is self-focused, but it helps us de-stress, sleep better, and have more energy. Meditation is self-focused, but it helps us become more accepting, emotionally regulated, and patient. Taking a power nap might be self-focused, but it also might recharge us so that we can cook a good meal for our loved ones.

We can take care of ourselves without becoming self-absorbed. But we need to view our self-care as an investment rather than an owed debt. To make this shift, I use a concept I call "ripples of influence."

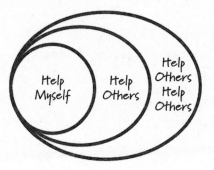

There are times when we live in the first ripple: helping ourselves. But we can help ourselves with a focus on rippling outward to the next level: helping ourselves so we can help others.

For example, grading essays sucks a lot of time from an English teacher's life. In the midst of grading a pile of papers, this teacher might think that he deserves a break. Then he may reframe it as "I need a break because life owes me one" and then play a video game for 20 minutes. Instead, he could reframe his thoughts to consider what self-reward will help him help others: "I'm going to go walk my dog and reset my brain so I can be present and intentional with my feedback for round two."

We can even apply this approach to our professional development and adjusting our strategies: *Am I doing X just to make my life easier? Or can I try Y to make my life easier so I can be a better teacher for my students?*

Reframing *why* I'm focusing on myself changes *what* I do to take care of myself.

Life Assignments

The core of the approach to altruism described in this chapter is maintaining focus on the end goal: making another person's life better. We *give* our best when we're *at* our best. And being an educator is about giving our best. It's time to take our giving to a new level. Here are some assignments to do just that.

Assignment #1:
Set Up an Altruism Fund

An act of kindness doesn't have to cost money. But the love is easier to spread with a little cash, right? We know that teachers are already altruistic in their personal spending on students. Give your personal bank accounts a break and create a class altruism fund.

Throughout the year my students and I raise money in small and large ways for our positive psychology fund. Aside from using these funds to go on service trips and get class materials, we use the money to spread kindness. Sometimes a student group will come to me unexpectedly with an idea. Other times, I challenge groups to come up with kind ways to spend a chunk of money. Here are some of the ways my students have decided to use the money:

- Get the school custodian a gift card for dinner and a baseball game.
- Buy donuts to randomly hand out in the hallway.
- Pay for random students' lunches.
- Clear a balance for a lunch account that a student can't pay.
- Buy a student a specific book to stoke his passion.
- Place a small, unexpected gift on a student's desk before she comes into class.
- Send flowers to a teacher who is sick or injured.

How to raise money? There are endless ways to get cash, but here are a few that have worked for us:

- **Host a can-collection contest.** Pit your classes against each other (or a colleague's) to see who can collect and deposit the most cans from their neighborhood. Sometimes the folks who run your sports concession stands will let you collect at an event.
- **Sell T-shirts.** Find a local T-shirt company that will give you a good deal. One group of mine sold shirts that said "Spread Positivity" in cool lettering. In three weeks, they raised more than $500 for our fund.
- **Sell snacks or beverages.** Depending on your school's policies, you might be able to sell small goods from your class or common area. I sell coffee in the mornings to keep our fund (and my energy) well stocked.
- **Volunteer for concession stands.** Some schools (including local colleges) allow groups to work concession stands to earn money.
- **Conduct a penny war.** A classic penny war (see how many pennies you can collect) is another easy way to get some quick cash. Either host it schoolwide or between classes or grade levels.
- **Make a holiday gift request.** Ask your family and friends to donate to your class fund for your birthday or other events. It's the gift that keeps on giving.

Assignment #2:
Initiate a Week of Kindness

There's a great scene in the TV show *The Good Place* in which Michael (Ted Danson) explains the point system for how to make it to heaven (or how to go the other route). Scrolling across the screen are dozens of items and points, such as positive points for remembering a sibling's birthday and remaining loyal to your football team and negative points (hundreds of thousands of points) for committing genocide.

Humor aside, I love the idea of making life about doing more good than bad. The effects of good (and bad) can't be quantified, but why not use a point system to encourage doing more good?

If numbers motivate you, attach a point system to each item in Appendix C: 75 Altruistic Acts for Educators. See how many points you can rack up in a day or a week. Or get a group of "active altruists" together and have a friendly competition. If the idea of quantifying good detracts from the experience, or if competing against others turns you or others into a vicious opponent, then use the list to get ideas on how to help others—no points attached.

Assignment #3:
Plan a Day of Kindness

Creating a week of kindness can stuff our week with good vibes; however, doing a series of kind acts in one day creates bigger boosts in well-being than spacing them out (Lyubomirsky & Della Porta, 2012). Rather than hoping for random acts of kindness, plan intentional acts of kindness for a whole day. For example, think in the following categories:

- My kind act for a colleague will be _____.
- My kind act for a family member will be _____.
- My kind act for a stranger I will see at [location] will be _____.
- My kind act for a student will be _____.

Assignment #4:
Conduct a "Prospiracy"

In my positive psychology class, I have student mentors who help lead small groups. One of the challenges I give each mentor is to create a "prospiracy" for someone in their group who could use a boost. You're familiar with *conspiracies*, which are organized, secret commitments to do wrong. A *prospiracy* keeps the organized secrecy part but swaps evil for good.

For example, one mentor decided to leave a positive note and a favorite candy bar on a peer's desk. Unable to identify the "prospirator," the student decided to pay it forward. For a month, I watched this prospiracy cascade as students paid it forward anonymously. Prospiracies are great because they catalyze "positive paranoia." When a person doesn't know who is behind an act of good, anyone or everyone could be the benefactor.

Organize a prospiracy. Gather a group of people, choose a target, and get sneaky. I've seen some schools where teachers nominate a "boost student." For a prescribed span of time, staff members try to do subtle things to boost that student's day—from smiling at the student in the hallway to striking up a conversation about a favorite hobby. Stay low-key though; just as conspiracies are no fun after the reveal, prospiracies can get weird if it's too obvious what's happening.

Revisit the "ripples of influence" graphic that appears earlier in this chapter. The outer ripple brings us back to the immense power of cascading kindness: how do we help others help others?

This chapter is ultimately about helping more than just ourselves. My recommendation is that you invite others into your effort to do good. I encourage you to reframe how your teaching and your lessons can be about not only helping a student graduate, but also helping a child learn the skills and compassion necessary to do good in the world. Consider how every day you get a chance to help others learn to help others—indirectly, by watching you; and directly, by the tasks, the challenges, and the opportunities you give them.

Being the change we want to see in the world is a good way to live. But being the change, modeling the change, and teaching the change is better, for ourselves, our students, and our world. It's why we teach.

Action: Crafting Your Calling

Between stimulus and response there is a space.
In that space is our power to choose our response.
In our response lies our growth and our freedom.

—Unknown

Imagine if you could look at your class and know the future job of every student—not what the students *say* they want to be (veterinarian, YouTube star, rapper, video gamer, another veterinarian), but what they will actually *do* for work as adults. You would see future engineers, electricians, hair stylists, and house cleaners. Now predict which students will find the most meaning and engagement in their work. Which students will have a meaningful job? The doctor? The social worker? What about the custodian or the secretary? The gardener?

Our culture is obsessed with the idea of meaningful work—finding it, recognizing it, studying it. In the field of education, it's evident as we toss around statements like "I'm in it for the outcomes, not the income," as if the notion that teaching as meaningful work is automatic.

Despite the ubiquitous view of education as meaningful work, we all know the truth: the demands, the changes, and the challenges of teaching can abrade our sense of meaning. How many colleagues have you had who felt teaching had lost its meaning? How many times have *you* felt that this work had lost its meaning?

The characterization of teaching as a calling, coupled with the challenges of keeping that purpose, reveals that there are no guarantees for meaningful work. Yet society assumes that some fields create instant callings, whereas others are domains of drudgery.

We often misunderstand the relationship between meaning and work because there's more to having purposeful employment than finding the right fit. Research in the field of positive organizational scholarship is showing that the type of work does not guarantee the level of meaning and fulfillment. Instead, meaning can be *cultivated* by the ways in which workers craft their tasks, their relationships, and their perspectives on work, even in unexpected work domains.

We shouldn't assume that our meaning is set in stone once that work contract is signed. And we shouldn't give up on rediscovering the reasons teaching gave us a sense of purpose when we started. We can craft our own calling.

To better understand how our choices affect our meaning—and to reinvigorate our sense of purpose in the troughs of teaching—we need to talk about a couple dozen administrative assistants, a gardener, and some custodians.

A Job, a Career, or a Calling?

Teenagers are under immense pressure to "figure their lives out" during the awkward, volatile phase known as adolescence. I hear from my students how stressed they are about figuring out their "10-year plan," their college major, their life track. They can barely pick out an outfit without second-guessing themselves, let alone a college track that may lock them into a career with a meager average salary of $30,000.

It's important to me that my students—as products of our society's misguided views on meaningful work—understand a couple of things:

- Meaningful work is not exclusive to doctors, nonprofit staffers, and social workers. People find meaning in diverse occupations.
- Try to find your calling while understanding that not every person will find one. It's OK if we have to work in a job that doesn't fit our bill as a "calling" in order to play and serve others.

This last point in particular is explored with a simple assignment that I give my students. I ask them to interview people about whether they consider their work a job, a career, or a calling. The results students find from this task—and the research on which it's based—can shift our view of how people cultivate meaning in their work.

Researchers asked 196 employees from diverse fields to describe their work and job satisfaction (Wrzesniewski, McCauley, Rozin, & Schwartz, 1997). Occupations ranged from computer programmers to nurses to educators, and incomes spread from less than $25,000 a year (39 percent of respondents) to more than $75,000 a year (3 percent of respondents). Participants responded to scenarios and survey questions designed to see if they considered their work a job (done for money and basic needs but not fulfilling), a career (mainly focused on advancement), or a calling (enjoyable, fulfilling work). Any predictions on the results?

The researchers found a few interesting things. First, workers were split in nearly perfect thirds as to whether they viewed their work as a job, a career, or a calling. As many of us would predict, the higher the pay and prestige of the job, the more likely a person was to describe the work as a calling. But here's the plot twist: a group of administrative assistants surprised researchers. The 24 of them—all of whom had similar demographics and work requirements—were again evenly split as to whether they considered their work a job, a career, or a calling. In other words, the type of work alone does not dictate whether one finds meaning and fulfillment.

When my students survey people about their work, they find similar surprises. They find bus drivers who have callings and managers who have jobs. They find teachers who have careers *or* jobs *or* callings. Some of my students found a person who changed their view of work and meaning altogether: a gardener.

"I will probably remember her forever," a student wrote in an e-mail message. She was reflecting on one of our altruism trips. She and a group of students approached a gardener who was toiling away in isolation. They asked about her work and expected her to describe it as a job—something she did for money. To these students, gardening did not fit the "image" of a calling. Not only did the gardener's answer surprise these students, but for some, it resonated far beyond the trip.

Despite the fact that she was the only person in charge of Bronson Park, a large central park in Kalamazoo, she said her work was her calling. Her focus went beyond planting, watering, and weeding; beyond making the park look good. Her focus was on caring for both the park and the people in it.

This park is notorious for being a central hangout for homeless people. The gardener described at length how important it is to her to connect with the displaced, to interact with these people, to *treat* them as people. She knows all their names and she knows how much they care about her and the park, too. On multiple occasions they've stopped vandals from damaging the park because they know how important the gardener's work is to her. And her ultimate goal is to build tiny houses, because in her words, "If they don't have a house, they don't have a place for a paycheck to be sent; so how can they start gaining stability?"

The gardener's answer to the question of work resonated with my students. And it reveals something deep and complex about the relationship between meaning and work. We know that meaning can be found in any occupation. But from where does it emerge? Does our engagement, our purpose, our happiness depend on finding the *right* work? Is it up to us to change how we *feel* about our work? Or is it something else? (Hint: it's something else.)

Three Doors on the Route to Meaningful Work

There's often a battle between the "uppers" and the "lowers" on the work ladder over the route to meaningful work. Upper management often chooses door number one, expressed with the directive "Deal with it." Picture the crotchety upper-crust CEO bemoaning how workers should stop griping, be grateful, and change perceptions in order to get more out of work.

The workers yap that the solution is door number two, which asserts that if those in charge would change work tasks and conditions, then work would be more meaningful. As images of historical labor battles flash into your mind, you know that this debate has existed for as long as ... well, as long as work has existed.

Regardless of what camp you fall into, we face a reality: the debate over how to create "ideal" working conditions will persist, while workers still work and managers still try to get workers to work differently.

So what do we do in the meantime? We do what the gardener did. We choose door number three. We craft our jobs to alter tasks, cultivate relationships, and reframe importance. We don't simply wait for meaningful work. We make meaningful work by crafting our calling.

Crafting a Calling

Think back to that summer job you had when you were a student. What did you do to make it more enjoyable? You probably did several things. Maybe you changed who you interacted with and how. You avoided that annoying, gossipy coworker and signed up for shifts with your friend. Perhaps you altered the work tasks themselves, volunteering to take cleaning duty or cashier responsibilities instead of flipping burgers.

Psychologists call this "job crafting." Job crafting is what employees do to redesign their work in order to foster engagement, satisfaction, resilience, and thriving (Wrzesniewski & Dutton, 2001). Beyond summer gigs, you've probably practiced job crafting as a teacher to some degree, whether you know it or not.

Researchers Amy Wrzesniewski (Yale School of Management) and Jane Dutton (University of Michigan) have interviewed employees in a variety of occupations. They've found that everyone crafts jobs in some way. For example, in interviewing hospital custodians, they found workers who walked elderly visitors back to their cars so the patient wouldn't worry about them getting lost. Another rearranged the décor in coma wards, believing that the change in environment might spur recovery. They did this despite the fact that these tasks weren't in their job description, and they risked being fired for doing them (Wrzesniewski, 2014).

Although we all make choices that affect our engagement at work, signs point to the benefits of job crafting more frequently and intentionally. Workers who describe their work as meaningful stand as positive members of organizations. Compared to those who just describe their work as a job, "calling" folks identify more as a team, have less conflict, trust their organization more, and have more positive communication with their colleagues (Wrzesniewski, 2003).

Interventions designed to teach job-crafting skills to Fortune 500 workers have yielded positive results as well. Compared to a control group, workers who intentionally job-crafted more than the control group increased their work effectiveness and happiness as reported by their managers and colleagues (Center for Positive Organizations, 2018).

As a teacher, you've done what you could to alter the tasks you teach, the projects you take on. You've made choices to change your interactions with colleagues, parents, and students. You've done some basic crafting. Let's take those crafting skills to a new level. But before we go smashing and reassembling that occupation of yours, let's process your need for purpose.

Using Introspection to Guide Job Crafting

The gurus of job crafting identify three categories to guide crafting efforts (Berg, Dutton, & Wrzesniewski, 2013):

- **Motives**—What drives you to put in effort and persistence? Is it the desire to help someone through an adversity? Is it the need to contribute something lasting?
- **Strengths**—What are you good at? What are your weaknesses?
- **Passions**—What sparks a deep interest in you? What problems and tasks do you find yourself deeply absorbed in?

To help myself craft teaching into a true calling, I modify these three categories into five:

- **Top-Level Goal**—What is my "teaching thesis?" What is the most important, long-term focus of my teaching?
- **Boosts**—What makes me love this job?
- **Burdens**—What frustrates me about this job?
- **Gifts**—What are my strengths?
- **Gaps**—What are my weaknesses?

Here's a sample of some of the ways I've revamped my boosts, burdens, gifts, and gaps:

Top-Level Goal: Use education, authentic relationships, and social psychology to help people cultivate purpose, perspective, and perseverance.

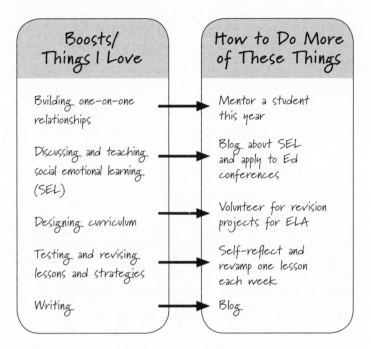

Boosts/Things I Love

- Building one-on-one relationships
- Discussing and teaching social emotional learning (SEL)
- Designing curriculum
- Testing and revising lessons and strategies
- Writing

How to Do More of These Things

- Mentor a student this year
- Blog about SEL and apply to Ed conferences
- Volunteer for revision projects for ELA
- Self-reflect and revamp one lesson each week
- Blog

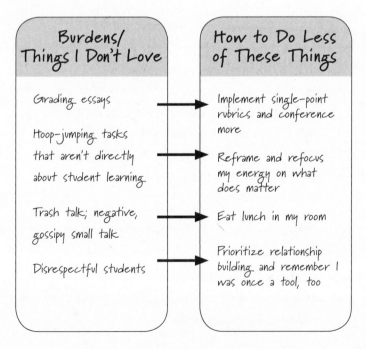

Burdens/Things I Don't Love

- Grading essays
- Hoop-jumping tasks that aren't directly about student learning
- Trash talk; negative, gossipy small talk
- Disrespectful students

How to Do Less of These Things

- Implement single-point rubrics and conference more
- Reframe and refocus my energy on what does matter
- Eat lunch in my room
- Prioritize relationship building and remember I was once a tool, too

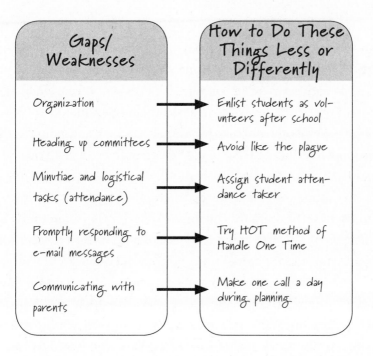

Assessing your top-level goal and your boosts, burdens, gifts, and gaps illuminates what is shining or shadowy about your work. Once you've taken some time to reflect on each, consider two critical principles to guide your effort to craft a calling: (1) focusing on an internal locus of control, and (2) the power of a 5 percent shift.

Principle #1: Focusing on an Internal Locus of Control

First, acknowledge that you're capable of crafting your work, even in minor ways. Researchers liken this to having a growth mindset for your work (Berg et al., 2013). Although many people believe that their work is fixed, job crafters believe that they're capable of creating shifts. Even if you have strict expectations and requirements, remember that people all over the world have crafted their work and continue to make shifts no matter what the context.

Nevertheless, we often get stuck in a belief that satisfaction and engagement at work is beyond our control. We often feel as though we're in a vise: on one side is societal, legislative, and administrative pressure; on the other is the often challenging state of our students, whose home life, temperament, and genetics are beyond our control. How do we establish autonomy to craft our job when there are so many things that we have to do and so many we can't? We must cultivate an internal locus of control.

My students quickly learn to stop asking questions such as "Do we have to write this down?" My response is automatic and consistent: "The only thing you have to do is make a choice. Some choices move us forward; other choices hold us back."

The response stems from my commitment to fighting "have-to-itis," a debilitating cognitive disease in which people ignore their autonomy. Students aren't the only ones susceptible to have-to-itis. Adults catch it too. How often have you heard (or made) statements like these?

- Ugh! I have to go to a staff meeting after school.
- Sorry, it's school policy so I have to follow the rule.
- We have to cover this because it will be on the test.

In James Hunter's book *The Servant*, individuals discuss the role of choice in leadership (and in life). Someone brings up the adage: "There are only two things you have to do in life: Die and pay taxes." After some deliberation, they realize that this adage is false: We don't *have* to pay taxes. But if we don't there are consequences. In reality, one person quips, "[T]here are only two things you have to do. You have to die and you have to make choices" (Hunter, 2012, p. 161).

Choice is the heart of autonomy—and humanity. We don't *have* to go to a staff meeting. We choose to go or not to go. But we accept the consequences—positive or negative. We don't have to follow a school policy. But our choice to do so or not do so leads to consequences. Every time we attribute our actions to "having" to do something, we relinquish our locus, or center, of control.

A large body of research focuses on the difference between an internal locus of control and an external locus of control. My colleagues at the Quantum Learning Network, however, helped me understand not just what the differences are, but how they show up in behavior.

For example, say that you're in the situation I was in recently. Administrators request that the teaching staff hold students more accountable for using technology appropriately (e.g., not using cell phones to text in the middle of class). Imagine you have slacked on cell phone accountability (as I had). What would your response be?

External Locus of Control Behaviors

1. **Blame.** Attribute a circumstance solely to someone else. *I wouldn't have a problem with cell phones in class if parents actually held their kids accountable at home.*

2. **Justify.** Excuse negative behavior because others are doing it or we don't think it matters. *Even if I tighten up, they'll get away with it in other classes.*

3. **Deny or lie.** *If they ask during an observation, I can just tell my administrators that I gave the student consequences after class ended.*

4. **Quit.** *Whatever. If admin think it's such a big problem, they can write me up for it. I care about more important things.*

Internal Locus of Control Behaviors

1. **Own our choices.** *I have loosened my standards and let too many kids bend the rules. I haven't been as consistent in holding them accountable as I could be.*

2. **Own the consequences of our choices.** *(A) Several factors make accountability for technology hard, but my choice*

to do nothing doesn't make it any easier or better. (B) I can't
control what parents or teachers in other classes do, but I can
influence the culture in my classroom.

There is a far larger conversation and there are many teachable moments contained within this brief overview of locus of control. However, from a crafting standpoint, we should know that there are benefits to focusing on our choices rather than justifying or blaming others.

For example, a study of 774 healthcare workers found that those with an internal locus of control were more likely to use problem-solving strategies and therefore less likely to experience psychological strain at work (Dijkstra, Beersma, & Evers, 2011). A meta-analysis of worker performance and relationship traits found that internal locus of control is one of the best traits for job satisfaction and job performance (Judge & Bono, 2001). And a study of more than 300 teachers in high- and low-stress schools found that educators with an internal locus of control felt less stress, resulting in better relationships with students, administrators, and parents and fewer discipline problems and conflicts (Parkay, Greenwood, Olejnik, & Proller, 1988).

Later in this chapter, we'll look at ways to reframe our thoughts for a more internal locus of control. For now, before you begin crafting your calling, focus on the choices you can make (which are many) rather than the factors beyond your control.

Principle #2:
The Power of a 5 Percent Shift

A second principle for crafting your calling is simple: use the power of a 5 percent shift. Don't overwhelm yourself with overhauling your entire job. When confronted with a large undertaking, it's important to shift your mindset to what Cornell researcher Karl Weick (1986) calls "small wins." To do this, think in terms of a 5 percent shift: *How do I shift 5 percent of my time and energy to make my work more meaningful?*

Maybe that shift involves having a student helper take attendance first thing so you can have more meaningful interactions with students at the start of class. Perhaps you invest a small chunk of time during lunch to respond to a few e-mail messages so that you can spend more time after school mentoring a student or colleague.

I shifted a couple of writing-skill review lectures to digital downloads, freeing up more time for writing conferences with students. Not only do I find it more meaningful to talk one-on-one with my students, but it also cuts down on time spent on the most painful task of an English teacher's work: grading essays. I've found that small shifts in how I manage lessons, logistics, or time have a larger ripple effect on my engagement, satisfaction, and sense of meaning.

As with any change in habit or behavior, take little steps. Start with a 5 percent (or even a 1 percent) shift toward more meaningful tasks and relationships.

Life Assignments

With an understanding of where you stand, as well as a dedication to owning your choices and making small wins in your role, explore the three main methods for crafting your calling, or what I call the "crafting trifecta": changing the *what*, the *who*, and the *why*.

Assignment #1: Craft the *What*

One of the main ways people change their interaction is through "task crafting": changing the number, scope, or type of job tasks (Wrzesniewski & Dutton, 2001). I call this "crafting the *what*." Here are some ways to do this.

Develop a new task. I know, I know. *More work*? Although we're already strapped for time, I've noticed two things whenever I've taken on new tasks like creating electives, sponsoring clubs, or spearheading committees. First, I've learned that when pressed, I can be far more efficient with other tasks that "demand" my time. If I know I have only 30 minutes to respond to e-mail messages before my club meets, then I'm efficient (e.g., I don't *need* to check social media feeds between messages). Second, taking on a task I love and find important is fuel. My passions, strengths, and motives are so engaged that energy reverberates throughout the rest of my work. There is a reason that researchers find a positive relationship between one's calling and one's work performance (Berg et al., 2013).

Renew a task. We also don't have to start tasks from scratch. We can reallocate, shifting our time emphasis to the things we value. For example, evaluating written work is a time drain for me. Depending on my schedule, assigning a single written task sometimes results in taking home 90-plus essays to review. So I started using single-point rubrics for more efficient feedback. Not only did this new approach reduce the time I spent at home on a burdensome task but it also allowed me more time for my boost: creating lesson plans and curriculum.

Consider a task that is both dreadful and time consuming. Then consult your tribes or online sources to modify the task to be 5 percent more efficient without compromising quality.

Outsource. Don't just pick up meaningful tasks. Let go of tasks that you don't love. You know which classroom task I can't stand? Organizing and cleaning. I'm that teacher who doesn't notice the random, unerased lines on my whiteboard. So what do I do? I find the kids who can't stand them and channel their passion for order.

Think about your own situation. What is one annoying task that someone else could do?

Do a side hustle. My "uppers" and gifts have a few overlapping opportunities: creating, writing, and speaking. Sadly, creative control and expression can be limited with common curricula and teaching assignments. So I've spent years developing opportunities to create, write, and speak as a side hustle. Whether that meant writing a blog for educators (www.affectiveliving.com) or cultivating speaking skills through keynote addresses, teacher trainings, and school presentations, I've learned the value of finding meaningful work that stretches beyond my daily classroom.

What's that *thing* you'd love to do that your job doesn't allow? Beyond summer or winter vacations, how can you carve out a sliver of time to develop that task? Again, use the power of a 5 percent shift. I made a goal of cutting down my video-binging by 30 minutes each night and reading or writing instead. Dedicating just 30 minutes to a task you love—even if it has nothing to do with education—can make a world of difference to your sense of meaning.

Assignment #2: Craft the *Who*

Teaching is a social endeavor, so we have a lot of opportunities to practice "relational craft," a second type of job crafting (Wrzesniewski & Dutton, 2001). I call this "crafting the *who*."

Recharge that extrovert or introvert. Lunchtime is sacred for teachers. In this tiny window of time, we're able to recharge ourselves. For some, this entails going to the lounge for some quality interaction with other adults. For me, it entails two things: getting away from people and blasting some soul music in my classroom.

It took me years to realize how important it was for me to spend time away from people—or at least get away from the draining trash talk found in many teacher lounges. Although there are moments when I choose to build connections with colleagues, relational crafting for me, an introvert, looks like decompressing to reflect and blaring some D'Angelo tunes.

If you're an extrovert, use spare moments to connect with positive, constructive people. If you're an introvert, do what you need to do for yourself. We have limited time in our day as educators. Use each second with purpose to craft more meaning.

Mentor someone. We get into education to help kids. We often get out of education because the tasks, the conversations, and the decisions make us lose sight of helping kids. But no matter how much the individuality of a child is lost in the noise, we can silence the din and invest in a kid by serving as a mentor.

Mentoring has kept me in education. No other choice has been more meaningful and motivating than building relationships with and helping individual students. There are many programs in schools and beyond that provide opportunities to mentor students. But we can also create meaningful interactions through what I call "ninja-favoritism."

The term *favoritism* is controversial, I know. A teacher would never have favorites, right? Bah! We know that we *do* have favorites because we're human. We're also professionals who don't diminish the education of students just because we don't like them—no matter how hard that is.

I therefore don't suggest *shunning* kids. I'm talking instead about ninja-favoritism—finding subtle ways to increase your connection with specific kids in ways that don't trigger cries of disproportion from their peers. Use breaks between classes, at lunchtime, and before and after school to build relationships with kids who inspire a sense of purpose. Ninja-favoritism doesn't mean favoring the "good" kids. Some of my most rewarding relationships emerged when I invested in some of my most challenging students.

Assignment #3: Craft the *Why*

A third type of crafting is often known as "cognitive crafting": changing the cognitive task boundaries. Often this means shifting to see the *whole* of our work's purpose instead of the individual parts (Wrzesniewski & Dutton, 2001). I consider this changing how we frame the *why* behind teaching.

Post your teaching thesis. A teaching thesis is not the same as a dreaded doctoral dissertation. It's an articulation of why you teach. Similar to a top-level goal, researchers find that cognitive crafters identify the whole of what their work is designed to do (Berg, Dutton, & Wrzesniewski, 2007).

A teaching thesis is a specific version of this. It answers the question "Why do I choose to teach?" For example, my teaching thesis—the *why* statement for my teaching—is this:

> I teach to cultivate authentic relationships to help young adults build the perspective, perseverance, purpose, and skills they need to flourish in their lives.

A framed version of this thesis sits on my desk so I can check myself any time I'm drained, any time the conversation with colleagues shifts to "students as standardized scores," any time the heavy burden of building better readers weighs me down. In other words, when I'm lost in the *parts* of my job, I cue myself to remember the *big picture*.

What's your purpose for teaching? And how can you keep this purpose present and tangible in your classroom? Maybe it's a note on your desk or a background image on your computer screen. Use concise words or a visual image to remember why you do what you do.

Sort the majors from the minors. I spent eight of my grade school years at a Catholic school. One of my key takeaways from grade school is that Catholics love rituals. Genuflecting. Sitting. Standing. Reciting. Sitting. Standing. Reciting. I can't remember a whole lot of *what* I recited a bajillion times, but one prayer has always held strong in shaping my purpose—the serenity prayer. Even though the prayer, written by American theologian Reinhold Niebuhr, doesn't have an official connection with Catholicism,

I remember hearing and saying it over and over at various times throughout my adolescence:

> God grant me the serenity to accept the things I cannot change, the courage to change the things I can, and the wisdom to know the difference.

That concept—of sifting through what is within or beyond my influence—has helped me craft my calling.

A lot of things in education are beyond our control. Yet we give those things space in our minds, ruminating and raging about them. In such moments, I make a cognitive shift toward the purposeful things within my control. I do this by turning the serenity prayer into a practice: I write about the things beyond my immediate control, link them to things I can control, and reconfigure the two (sometimes just in my mind) into actions or tasks that are meaningful and within my realm of influence. Here are some examples:

Beyond my control: The parenting history of my students

Within my control: Communication with parents

Meaningful and within my realm of influence: Having debriefing conversations to inform parents and teach students life skills

Beyond my control: State mandates (e.g., frequency of state testing)

Within my control: Assessing students

Meaningful and within my realm of influence: Empowering students with skills and feedback

Beyond my control: Administrative rules (e.g., cell phone policy)

Within my control: Monitoring technology use

Meaningful and within my realm of influence: Designing clear and consistent ways for students to use technology for intellectual development

Beyond my control: What's on the SAT
Within my control: Lesson orchestration
Meaningful and within my realm of influence: Creating lessons that engage students and build conceptual knowledge

Every frustration beyond our control can be cognitively reframed into a purposeful action step. We just need the courage and the wisdom to see the difference.

Focus on service. Throughout the many years I've spent exploring meaning in my personal life and with my students, one constant has always remained: actions are meaningful when they positively affect others. This anchor of service, which was outlined in Chapter 8, can be used to ground our cognitive crafting. We can especially use it to reframe the things we *don't* like to do in our jobs. Before taking on something I dread, I occasionally prompt myself with a question: "How will my actions help someone?" I've used this in a lot of different contexts, such as

- Before having a one-on-one conversation with a student about a plagiarized paper. (*This conversation can help empower a student to learn skills for working with integrity.*)
- Before calling a parent to discuss student behavior. (*My call will open a line of communication that will help me, the parent, and the student move forward.*)
- Before going into a staff meeting. (*By aligning with my colleagues, I'm helping my students have a more consistent and reliable education.*)
- Before striking up a conversation in the workroom with a venting colleague. (*She needs to feel heard by someone. My*

listening might help her release some stress before getting back to work with students.)

- Before starting to assess student work. (*Feedback is a critical part of learning. I'm not just grading; I'm helping a student learn.*)

I'm not naive enough to think that these reframings guarantee change for the other person; that venting colleague might still rage at the world no matter how actively I listen. But I do know that they help me engage more positively and meaningfully with my job.

Prompting ourselves to focus on service to others can change how we interact (Grant, 2007). It channels our energy into a positive, purposeful path of meaningful work.

Assignment #4: Shift from the Parts to the Whole

One major strategy that researchers use to help people job-craft is unifying the "parts" of job tasks into a meaningful "whole." For example, I have a tendency to see tasks such as promptly taking attendance, completing IEP data forms, and monitoring progress as disparate and superfluous—busywork or hoop-jumping. But I've learned how much these small details help my administrators and special education colleagues make more informed decisions to help my students. And because I value empowering others, I've learned to reframe these tasks as one whole:

~~Busy work~~ → Helping to empower my colleagues with critical information

When you feel frustrated (or bored) by the individual tasks, unify them under one larger whole—something at the core of what you value.

Your circumstances, your needs, and your frustrations may be different from mine. But stagnation is a choice, and discontent is a disease with many cures—many of which exist inside our own head. Crafting a calling is not the acceptance of poor work conditions; it's working to create better conditions for ourselves when others can't (or won't). It's a decision to *make* change rather than *wait* for change.

When I almost quit teaching a few years ago, a thought kept flickering in the darkness of my discontent: I need change. I was frustrated that others weren't making the changes I wanted. Despair led me to consider change by leaving the classroom altogether. Desire to cultivate this calling, though, made me pause and come to an important realization: I can change my circumstances without jumping ship. I can take control of my career rather than throwing in the towel as a victim of the system.

Throughout this book, I've credited each one of the awarenesses, attitudes, and actions with helping me personally thrive in education. But crafting a calling—more than any other efforts I've made—kept me in the classroom, doing what I know I was born to do.

If these techniques help you simply survive the year, good. If they help you make the most out of the next few years before you consider larger changes, great. And if they help you reignite and refuel your passion for education indefinitely, even better. Maintaining the fire for education hinges upon our choices—whether we let the flame burn out or take action to refuel.

10

Action: Ambitious Acts

Live as if you'll die tomorrow; learn as if you'll live forever.

—Unknown

Forty minutes from where I teach is a little town called Fennville, a farming community of 1,400 people that's an emblem of small-town Michigan. Kind. Reserved. Proud. Though Fennville isn't known for generating A-list celebrities, there is one person who had a profound impact on the community and a deep effect on me: Wes Leonard. I never met Wes Leonard, but his story changed my life.

Wes Leonard's reputation is built around two things: being a good person and being a great athlete. His junior year, he and the Fennville basketball team set out to do something seemingly impossible: have an undefeated season. In the final game of the season, with seconds left and the score tied 55 to 55, that opportunity teetered on the final play.

Fennville inbounds the ball, seeking their star athlete, Wes. He drives through the paint as players part like clouds. Wes lifts for a lay-up and Fennville takes the lead. The crowd, a majority of the town's population, goes wild. As the seconds tick and their defense holds strong, Fennville claims victory, completing a perfect season and priming the team for a state title run. His teammates lift Wes into the air, cheering their star player, their leader.

But then everything changes. Minutes later, as he goes to hug a teammate, he grips his chest and collapses. There is confusion as some scream for help and others are unaware of the crisis. Wes isn't responding. The frantic scurry for an automated external defibrillator (AED) is too late. Wes dies shortly after being rushed to the hospital. Sudden cardiac arrest from an enlarged heart. Sixteen years old.

Sixteen.

Every educator has known a child who died too soon, and every such tragedy affects us. But despite not knowing him, Wes's story hit me. He wasn't texting and driving. He wasn't barreling too fast down country roads. He wasn't abusing drugs or alcohol. He wasn't even playing sports against medical orders; no one even knew he was susceptible to cardiac arrest. His life simply ended too soon.

What shook me most about Wes's death was a sobering fact: we don't know when our lives will end. We may eat the right foods, treat our bodies well, take our annual check-ups seriously, but life is not guaranteed. Life is fragile.

And yet we treat life as if the median of mortality is contractual, telling ourselves there is another time, another year, another tomorrow. In doing so, we drift along, without either strong aims or the urgency to go after the things we want. We make casual references to things we'd like to do and then slink back into the mindless waves of watching television and scrolling social media feeds. We often tell our students to begin with the end in mind. But what about telling ourselves to *live* with the end in mind?

Wes Leonard's story has pushed me to stop drifting and start steering toward the things I want, professionally and personally. In the process, I've learned a great deal about how goals—setting them and making progress toward reaching them—affect well-being. My learning comes from both research on accomplishment and my own experience of developing and dedicating myself to a bucket list.

This chapter focuses on using the urgency of mortality to set goals we want to achieve to enhance our well-being—living with the end in mind. We'll look at the research behind goals—big goals, small goals, goals that stretch us, goals that help others, goals that enliven us, and even goals that have nothing to do with the classroom. If you have goals, this chapter will give you the tools and strategies to reach them more consistently. If you don't have many goals, well, you owe it to your well-being to set some. Start by becoming a "lister."

Becoming a Lister

The end *was* on my mind as I contemplated my probable and tragic death as a result of being crushed by an elephant, half a world away from my wife and home. I was doing something I never thought I'd be able to do: riding an elephant beside the ruins of Buddhist temples in Thailand.

I sat 12 feet above the ground atop a lumbering Asian elephant. I looked at the deep ditch beside the dirt path. I listened to the soft murmurings of the man I thought of as "the elephant pilot," guiding the neo-dinosaur with aplomb. But I also saw the foot-long spike the guide held in his hand to be used if the elephant revolted. A slight shuffle to the left would send me and the other riders toppling to the ground—with a four-ton grey giant crushing us into dust.

When you grow up in a lower-middle-class family, you don't imagine yourself on elephants in faraway countries. My childhood vacations consisted of weekend trips to the local motel (highlights included cable TV and a chlorinated pool). I didn't grow up with the tastes and promises of wild ambitions and adventures.

So I floated in life the way I floated aimlessly in the motel pool. In other words, I grew up with vague dreams instead of concrete goals. Playing soccer, I wanted to win games. Junior year, I knew I wanted to be a teacher, so I had an obvious goal of graduating from college. When I enjoyed playing music, performing in front of people was a passive dream instead of a goal that I truly worked toward.

I didn't actively set goals until I met people through the Quantum Learning Network who had clear, written goals—people who acted on big goals. I became inspired by grand figures like John Goddard, who, at the age of 15, made a life list of 127 things. Among other things, he milked poisonous snakes, explored the Nile by canoe, and circumnavigated the world, eventually checking off 110 items on his list and making a career out of goal setting before he passed away ("One Man's Life of No Regrets," 1972).

I realized that if I wanted the most out of my life, I had to *know* what I wanted. So I became a lister.

Listing what we want to do in life is the best starting point if we want to make the most out of our lives. Start by writing down anything that follows phrases like "I would love to... ," "It would be cool to... ," or "I've always wanted to... ." Although this is a book for educators, give yourself permission to think about goals beyond the classroom. Always wanted to go sky diving? Write the goal down. Think it would be cool to write a book? Write the goal down. Want to learn how to play the piano? Write the goal down. Don't judge or critique or doubt the goal. Just write it down.

Then, pick one and *try*. Put a down payment on a skydiving trip. Open your computer and start writing. March down to the music room at school and touch the piano keys. Try.

Listing goals is the easy part. Trying is the hard part. But the *trying* is what shifts our well-being. Anyone who has become addicted to goal setting can tell you that striving toward a goal amplifies our experience, pushing us beyond our safe bubbles, encouraging us to take risks. But striving toward goals offers more benefits than simply expanding our comfort zone.

Why Striving for Goals Matters

Visualize your life *without* goals—not just written career goals, but any goal. Think of showing up to work without any plans of what you wanted to accomplish. Imagine getting into a relationship without any goal (it wouldn't last long).

Even if you weren't feeling "ambitious," you couldn't do much without a goal. For example, a lazy drive around in your car on a Sunday requires at least a subconscious goal of "casual putzing."

Social psychologist Eric Klinger refers to goals as the "linch-pin of psychological organization" (1998, p. 44). Goals organize our mental resources, drive our decision making, and give us a reason to get up in the morning. It's no surprise, then, that goal-striving is good for our well-being. Researcher Robert Emmons (1986) found that having goals—whether we have succeeded in achieving them—is associated with greater subjective well-being. One meta-analysis of 85 studies showed a significant association between striving toward goals and improved well-being (Klug & Maier, 2014).

Striving toward goals creates what researchers call an upward spiral. It goes like this:

- People with a positive self-regard are more likely to set goals that are personally meaningful.
- Setting personally meaningful goals is linked to higher well-being (Judge, Bono, Erez, & Locke, 2005).
- Setting personally meaningful goals is also linked to increased likelihood of accomplishing goals (Sheldon & Elliot, 1999).
- Accomplishing goals improves our self-regard.

Before you raise the "correlation isn't causation" argument, you should know that studies find goal-striving to be *causational* for well-being too. Compared to control groups, people who received even brief interventions on goal-setting and planning skills increased their well-being (MacLeod, Coates, & Hetherton, 2007).

If you feel guilty about setting personal goals when you're reading a book about teaching, realize that striving toward goals in one domain of life boosts happiness across other domains (Wiese & Freund, 2005). A goal beyond the classroom can translate to being a happier, better teacher in the classroom.

Before you write down "Goal: Be happy" and call it a day, recognize that not all goals have the same effect. If you're chasing the wrong route to well-being, you may attain an ill-crafted goal but feel dejected.

You need to understand how goals can be *guides* for your well-being—leading you in the right direction of both success and satisfaction. In fact, you can use the acronym GUIDES as a mental checklist to ensure that your goals are more likely to increase well-being:

Generative versus self-serving

Uplifting versus avoiding

Intrinsic versus extrinsic

Developmental versus destinational

Experiential versus possessional

Specific versus vague

Generative Versus Self-serving

Consider the following goals:

1. Raise $1,000 for a scholarship.
2. Save $1,000 to buy a new TV system.

Would I be happier buying a 415-inch HDL-LCD-XYZ TV with surround sound or giving money to some kid I'll probably never see again? Although a new entertainment system would be nice, goals that "give" yield greater well-being.

Researchers have found strong links between well-being and goals that are aimed at helping others. Generative strivings, which provide something positive for other generations or other people, predict well-being and higher positive affect compared with striving for status and power goals (Emmons, 1991). In national samples, higher levels of generative motives, behaviors, and traits contributed to heightened levels of psychological and social well-being (McAdams, de St. Aubin, & Logan, 1993; Ryff, 1989).

What's interesting about research on generative motives and goals is that it flies in the face of what we're told: humans are selfish. But go deeper into that evolutionary itch of humanity and we shouldn't be surprised. We're driven to carry on humanity. Helping others helps us build protective, supportive tribes but also ensures that future generations actually have a future. Studies have found that spending money on others makes us feel better than spending on ourselves. The boost of prosocial spending is cross-cultural, correlational, causational, can be seen in toddlers, and is measurable on our brains (Aknin et al., 2013; Dunn, Aknin, & Norton, 2014). Goals that *give* are superior to goals that *get*.

Uplifting Versus Avoiding

Consider the following goals:

1. Eat a vegetable with every meal.
2. Stop eating sweets.

Uplifting goals are ambitions framed around positive incentives or experiences, compared to avoidant goals, which focus on preventing negative consequences. One might think that how we word a goal doesn't matter, but studies show that our framing does matter. Rather than setting a goal to minimize or avoid bad things, frame your goals to increase good, positive actions.

Between 10 and 20 percent of the average person's goals are avoidant goals, but studies find these goals to be associated with worse psychological outcomes (Emmons, 1999). Medical patients, for example, who set avoidant goals were less likely to attain those goals, felt a greater sense of external pressure to achieve them, and had more physical health complaints over time (Elliot & Sheldon, 1998). And avoidant goals don't only affect our success and well-being; they can also affect relationships. In a sample of married couples, marital satisfaction was negatively related to how much a spouse framed goals as avoidant instead of uplifting (King & Emmons, 1991).

To be clear, many of these studies primarily show correlation. Maybe unhappy people set avoidant goals. But as we explored in Chapter 1, focusing on the positives of life—even ones we're striving toward—can create uplifting patterns that boost our well-being.

Intrinsic Versus Extrinsic

Consider the following goals:

1. Master a tech strategy to help my kids engage more with their reading.
2. Use a tech strategy so my administrator gives me a better evaluation.

"If every one of your colleagues were rated 'highly effective' on their evaluation, would that change your motivation?" My principal posed this question to me and another teacher I greatly admire. I didn't need to think long about my answer. Neither did my colleague.

"Not one bit."

The question was rooted in a common, yet fraudulent, idea about motivation and goal setting: carrots and sticks will help us achieve more and thus make us happier. The glaring issue with this mode of thinking was apparent in our answer: our intrinsic standards, values, and goals are what drive us. Think about your own experience. When has a "point boost" on an evaluation made you happier than having a meaningful teachable moment with a student?

Intrinsic goals not only engage deeper motivation; they also produce greater well-being compared to extrinsic goals. Studies show that intrinsic goals produce greater long-term effort and thus higher-level goal attainment (Sheldon & Elliot, 1999). Making progress on intrinsic goals is linked to greater well-being, whereas progress on extrinsic goals has no relationship to our happiness (Brunstein, Schultheiss, & Grässman, 1998; Sheldon & Kasser, 1998). Focusing on extrinsic goals is also associated with higher anxiety, depression, narcissism, and physical illness (Kasser & Ryan, 1996). As a result, the most effective goals and feedback are framed around what intrinsically motivates someone, whether teacher or student, not the threat or pressure of assessment and evaluation.

Developmental Versus Destinational

Consider the following goals:

1. Train to complete a triathlon to improve my willpower.
2. Complete a triathlon.

Have you ever solved the Rubik's Cube puzzle? Not this guy. I've been working at solving it on and off for more than a year. Someday there will come a moment when that aggravating block will be back in its original color-coordinated form. Will that moment boost my happiness for months to come? Probably not. My ambition for taking on that block of fury isn't about the destination. It's about developing one of my personal weaknesses (spatial reasoning) into a skill. It's about minor victories.

We should have long-term goals that drive us. But once we set the destination, we should shift our focus to the short-term steps and the process along the way. Focusing too much on the destination or goal as a source of happiness may let us down. For example, one study found that depressed children were more likely to set goals attached to final outcomes compared to nondepressed children, who set goals attached to making progress or learning skills (Street et al., 2004).

A meta-analysis of 85 studies found that the benefits of having goals was significantly larger when people focused on goal progress instead of goal attainment (Klug & Maier, 2014). Setting process goals also encourages us to note short-term benchmarks. Aim for goals that are about developing ability and short-term progress.

Experiential Versus Possessional

Consider the following goals:

1. Drive Route 66.
2. Upgrade my Honda to a new BMW.

You've seen the Black Friday videos—people mauling each other for the latest must-have fuzzy robot. You've seen the growing lines outside electronics stores, extending like mold. People are obsessed with *stuff* and are willing to go through gauntlets for shiny things. Worse than the time wasted in line is a simple fact: spending on things is not as beneficial to our well-being as spending on experiences.

Sometimes our goals revolve around acquiring material possessions or things to bring us joy (and anyone who uses retail therapy understands the mood boost from a new purchase). However, in the long run, money spent on experiences yields greater gain for our life satisfaction (Hajdu & Hajdu, 2017). The rationale is multifaceted: experiences typically don't elicit as much social comparison as possessions, they often allow us to share with others, and they're often a more meaningful part of our identity (Caprariello & Reis, 2013). People even derive more happiness *anticipating* an experience compared to obtaining a possession (Kumar, Killingsworth, & Gilovich, 2014). If you're feeling the need to stand in line for a ridiculous amount of time, stand in line for theater tickets instead of toys. And make sure your goals are more about *doing* rather than *having*.

Specific Versus Vague

Consider the following goals:

1. Make someone smile.
2. Make someone happy.

In Chapter 8, I mentioned how, a few years ago, one of my student groups held a fundraiser selling T-shirts with a simple slogan: Spread Positivity. Our community loved them, and in merely two weeks the group raised more than $500 for intentional acts of kindness. Although the shirt sales were a success and the message is truly a great one, the effects of the slogan may be subpar. "Spread a Smile" might have generated a better mission for the T-shirt owner—at least according to a series of six Harvard studies.

The studies compared concretely framed goals, like "Make someone smile," to abstractly framed goals, like "Make someone happy." Participants who set concrete goals felt happier upon attempting their goal compared to the abstract-goal group (Rudd, Aaker, & Norton, 2014). The rationale was that the concrete goal was easier to verify in the mind of the goal-setter. The abstract goal, by contrast, may have created a larger sense of disappointment as the individuals wondered whether they really *did* make someone happy. Without a concrete piece of evidence, our expectations might cause an upward comparison and leave us disappointed.

Not only does setting a specific goal give us a better sense of satisfaction when we hit it; setting concrete goals, especially specific subgoals within a big, long-term ambition, can increase our likelihood of success (Locke & Latham, 2006).

Rather than "Improve my health," set a goal like "Complete a 5K." Rather than "Make someone's day," try something like "Buy a meal for someone."

Life Assignments

Now that you've got a good understanding of the importance of setting and striving toward goals—and what kinds of goals are actually worth pursuing—consider the following assignments to help you follow through on good intentions.

Assignment #1: Become a Lister

The most important step of any venture is the first step. Become a life lister. Open up a word processor, a journal, a note on your smartphone, a piece of paper—whatever resource you can return to again and again. Then start writing down some things you've always wanted to do.

Categorize goals under sections, such as Travel, Career, Family, Adventure, Fun, Health. Start with a simple target of writing down 20 goals; then see how momentum works to your advantage. Now is not the time for criticism (that time will come). Let your ambition loose and write anything and everything you want to do in life. If you like digital options, www.bucketlist.org is a great source for recording, finding, and sharing goals set by other "listers."

Think of a life list as a living document. You may add new goals, modify them, or even remove some goals that no longer interest you. Realize that for every one thing you check off your list, you may come up with a few more new goals. And that's a beautiful thing.

Assignment #2: Alert the Tribe

Want a great conversation starter? Post your life list somewhere visible. My list is posted on the back wall of my classroom, sparking conversations with my students almost daily. "You've seen the Dalai Lama in person?" "What's a 'Zombie 5K'?" "You haven't solved a Rubik's Cube yet!?" Believe me, nothing will hold you more accountable for reaching goals than fearing snarky criticism from youths.

Alerting the tribe is one way to hold yourself accountable. If public posting isn't your flavor, find an accountability partner—someone else who not only sets goals but goes after them. Or write your in-progress goal on the mirror in your bathroom, where you can be your own accountability partner.

Don't, however, get too lifted into the clouds, waxing poetic about your dreams. Some arguments and studies suggest that talking about goals can *lessen* our likelihood of accomplishing them (Sivers, 2010). To get the benefits of accountability without losing steam, read on.

Assignment #3: Don't Be Negative... or Naïve

You'd think with all my talk about goal setting and optimism that I would never falter on my goals, slaying New Year's resolutions left and right. False. I have a nemesis—a kryptonite—named "sugar." And it presents itself most potently in the form of glazed cake donuts with sprinkles. For years, no matter how resolute my diet plans, I would become hypnotized by the sweet trickery of donuts.

It seemed as though the world conspired against my goals. Every day en route to work, I pass by one of the top-ranked donut makers in Michigan. BOOM! Heavenly donuts for under a buck. Walk into school. BAM! Newspaper class is selling donuts for a fundraiser. Get to my classroom. WHAP! Kind-hearted students: "Here Mr. Mielke. We brought you a donut to show you how much we appreciate you."

My weakness changed, though, once I learned about the research-based practice of "mental contrasting with implementation intentions," better known as WOOP (see next page). The research addresses an interesting question: Who is more likely to succeed—the Pollyanna or the grouch? Though we might wager on the positive thinker, researchers realized that fantasizing about successful goals *demotivates* goal striving. And "glass half full" folks often underestimate the challenges accompanying ambitions.

But we also shouldn't bet on the grouches. Dispositional doubters often focus so much on the barriers, they don't even try. Researchers struck a balance between positive mindset and realistic barriers using WOOP, which stands for the following:

Wish—What do you want to accomplish? (Specify the goal.)

Outcome—What will you gain by completing the goal? (Visualize the benefits.)

Obstacle—What challenges might get in the way? (Identify barriers.)

Plan—How will you reduce or overcome these obstacles? (Prepare a response.)

For more background on WOOP, read Gabriele Oettingen's *Rethinking Positive Thinking* (2015) or peruse www.woopmylife .org. The gist of the strategy, however, is creating if/then plans: "If [obstacle], then I will [plan]."

Using if/then plans has helped me overcome my donut weakness more than any other goal-striving strategy. For example, I created these plans to battle the many barriers weakening my willpower:

- If I know driving past the donut shop will entice me, then I will take a different road to get to work.
- If kids are selling donuts in the school's common area, then I will follow a different route in the morning to get to my classroom.
- If students offer me a donut as a gift, then I will accept it gratefully and secretly give it away when they leave. (This last one is sketchy, I know, but effective.)

After choosing a life goal to tackle, be honest about your obstacles. But don't let the adversities stall you. Instead, come up with your responses ahead of time.

Assignment #4: Make a Grit Ladder

One of my more ambitious life goals was to finish a half-marathon. I *hate* running, but I knew pushing myself to do something I loathed would strengthen my willpower (another shout-out to process goals!). For months I hesitated to sign up until, just one week from race day, I decided to do it. Dumb, I know, to not train for a 13.1-mile run, but I was in it for the process, not the prize.

The first few miles felt easy. Then the suffering began. Every mile marker sparked a split-second panic of doubt and fear. What kept me going was refocusing. *Push for the next mile, don't stop.* Once I crossed that mile, I pushed for the next short-term marker. The last two miles I was setting hundred-yard goals. *Get to that street sign ahead. Get to the top of the hill. Push for 50 more steps.*

I finished—not in any Disney-esque surprise fashion, but I ran the whole time. That experience taught me a lot about mental strength (and the importance of training, as I struggled to walk for the next two weeks). It also taught me to strive for goals like a distance runner.

Distance runners are masters at balancing the long-term result with the short-term benchmarks. They have clear images of what the end goal looks like, but they pace themselves with smaller progress goals. Without those small markers, a runner might lose sight of the end goal or fail to pace.

There's been a lot of talk in education about grit and the importance of challenging, long-term goals. But we forget that all gritty goals are composed of multiple small goals, whether the goal is running a marathon, getting a doctorate, or taking a trip to Ireland. If we can break down the gritty goal into smaller phases, we can not only accelerate our pace but also fuel our motivation to keep striving.

A simple way to do this is to use what I call a "grit ladder." Map out a ladder, writing the gritty goal at the top. Then work backward to identify what major step is needed *right before* the end goal. Then consider: what must be done *before* that subgoal?

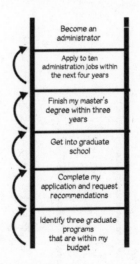

In addition to having an outline of what's necessary, the real focus is on figuring out a small goal we can accomplish this week in order to get one step closer. For example, rather than overwhelming myself with the cost of a trip to Ireland, I can focus on the short term: make coffee at home this week and put my latte money in a savings jar.

A built-in beauty of a grit ladder is getting frequent boosts of success. Our brains love a sense of completion, rewarding the success with a hit of the feel-good neurotransmitter dopamine. And dopamine drives addiction. Once the boost wears off, we crave the feeling. Fortunately, we have another manageable, short-term goal we can check off on the road to gritty glory. Grit ladders can fuel goal-striving addiction.

Bonus: this is a great strategy to use in the classroom. Check out a series of grit ladders that I borrowed from Olivia, my former student.

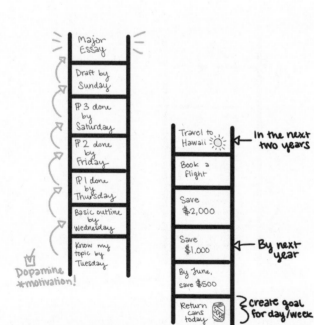

Walk the halls of my high school and you'll come across one of many metal boxes jutting out from the brick. Inside you'll find an AED. Outside the box you'll see the label "Wes Leonard Heart Foundation." The AEDs are a legacy of Wes Leonard, provided by the nonprofit that bears his name. I spot them each day, remembering not just the machine's function, but the young life that needed it. Wes Leonard's name lives on as a means not only to jump-start a struggling heart but also to jump-start our motivation in not taking life for granted.

Remember that life is fragile. The timeline is not guaranteed.

Stop floating in fantasies of what you'd *like* to accomplish. Take action. Set a goal that *guides* you toward well-being. Then start striving before it's too late.

Conclusion

The summer before my junior year in high school, I was ambling around a church book sale, neck stiffly tilted as I read the titles on the bindings. As in the rest of my life, I had no particular aim or interest I was trying to satisfy. I was just bored. But I spotted an intriguingly titled book: *The Art of Happiness,* by the Dalai Lama.

I attributed my curiosity to a desire to learn about Eastern philosophy. I now think there was, subconsciously, a bigger reason why I gravitated toward that book. I was struggling. And I was depressed.

In retrospect, I can't say whether it was the typical turmoil of adolescence or something more severe. But I know my outward behaviors masked how much I was suffering—the binge drinking, the getting kicked out of class, the gravitating toward mischief and rebellion. I swashed around between blaming others for my discontent and berating myself for inadequacy. And then I picked up that book with the picture of a smiling spiritual leader I knew nothing about.

To this day it is the only book that I can say completely changed my life. It left me with a powerful theme that is at the core of the book you hold: *our well-being is influenced by our actions, and our actions are a product of how we frame our thoughts.*

Though the text didn't kick the mischief out of me (nothing yet has), *The Art of Happiness* left a compass of self-direction that I would return to whenever I drifted. When I had a post-college breakup after a four-year relationship, I reread it. When I struggled to stay afloat during my challenging first years as a teacher, I reread it. Whenever I felt myself attaching my happiness to circumstances beyond my control, I revisited it.

It's no coincidence that my studying well-being also trails back to that book. I fell upon the field of positive psychology after reading *The Compassionate Instinct*, a collection of essays from gurus in the field (I read it because the Dalai Lama was a contributor).

A decade of studying the science of well-being has yielded the strategies and tools you've read about in this book. But it all goes back to that simple theme: *our well-being is influenced by our actions, and our actions are a product of how we frame our thoughts.*

Today, the theme of self-direction amidst external challenge is more necessary than ever. The circumstances of education are shifting, often adding more expectation, more tension, and less support. I see it daily. I feel it daily. You probably do too.

But the source most responsible for our well-being, our resilience, and our volition is us. When the mix of student behaviors in our classroom is tumultuous, we can rely on ourselves to not give up. When our weeks and months are filled with challenges, we can choose to find the opportunities to persevere. When we feel our emotions spinning out of control, we can ground ourselves back to our breathing. When adversarial ruminations stew in our minds, we can choose to let go of resentment. When we struggle, we can act.

With every awareness, every attitude, every action, we influence our state of well-being.

With every awareness, every attitude, every action, we influence the lives of our students.

We have power. Let's use it.

Appendix A:
Gratitude Lessons

As we all know, the best way to understand a concept is to teach it. I encourage every teacher to find ways to weave well-being lessons into students' school experience. Every practice described in this book has been taught and tested in my positive psychology class. These basic lessons on gratitude are frequently among my students' favorite lessons and practices.

Goal: Students will understand what gratitude is, why it matters, and how to cultivate it.

Enduring Understandings:

- Gratitude is the acknowledgment of good things and recognition that the source of good lies at least partially beyond ourselves.
- Comparing current happiness to how things could be better (upward hedonic contrasting) can diminish well-being and create envy.
- Comparing current happiness to how things could be worse (downward hedonic contrasting) can increase gratitude.

Key Questions:

- What is gratitude?
- Why does gratitude matter?
- What gets in the way of gratitude?
- How do we cultivate more gratitude?

Optimal Grade Levels: From 8th grade through postsecondary education

Introductory Lesson

1. Lead students with a discussion question: *How does social media affect our well-being?*

Elicit answers from students. Try to have students elaborate on examples of when social media has boosted or diminished their happiness. Guide them toward examples of when we might compare ourselves socially. I often ask students to explain to me the "culture of affirmation"—how the anticipation of likes, comments, or responses influences their interaction with social media.

2. Write "Hedonic Contrasting" on the board. With your students, define these terms:

- Hedonic contrasting—Mentally comparing our current level of happiness to how things could be.
- Upward contrasting—Comparing to how things could be *better*.
- Downward contrasting—Comparing to how things could be *worse*.

Elicit or share examples of each. I have students discuss things like the following:

- The weather (how we compare actual weather to how we think it should be).
- Following celebrities on social media.
- Examples from a school day (e.g., walking in the hallway).

Ask students how upward and downward contrasts can influence our happiness. Clarify that upward comparisons can be helpful for motivating ourselves sometimes, but they can also make us envious or feel worse about our lives. Downward comparisons can make us feel grateful and fortunate, but they can also make us feel guilty.

I try to help students focus on the idea that our mental comparisons are within our control. We can *choose* whether to make an upward or a downward comparison any time we want.

3. Segue to defining "gratitude." Introduce students to the concept of gratitude. You can pose the Key Questions for them to discuss before diving in with more depth.

After discussion, I have students write down the two components of gratitude:

- Acknowledging something good in our lives
- Recognizing that the source of good lies at least partially beyond ourselves

4. Outline and research the benefits of gratitude. I usually ask students to read the following article: *Gratitude Defined: Why Practice It?* (https://greatergood.berkeley.edu/topic/gratitude/definition#why-practice). The article gives an overview of gratitude, includes research on how it benefits us, and shares practices that boost gratitude. Be sure to read the article—and many of the suggested links—to expand your own understanding of the benefits, the limitations, and the approaches of gratitude.

Have students identify and reflect on (or discuss) one or two of the research findings that would most benefit their lives.

5. Reflect. Give students the challenge of coming to school the next day with examples of moments in which they used upward and downward hedonic contrasts. Ask them to reflect on two upward contrasts and two downward contrasts they made in the last 24 hours.

Gratitude Interventions

Here are a few of my students' favorite interventions. I strongly recommend you try each of these before asking students to do the same. Speaking from experience lends credibility. I do one of these interventions each Tuesday via "Gratituesday" (see Chapter 3).

The Gratitude Letter

1. Visualize. Have students take out a piece of paper. Have them think of a person who is still alive who has had a positive influence on their life. It might be helpful to have them close their eyes and walk them through a visualization, such as this:

> Imagine that you are seated next to this person on a park bench and it's your last chance to express your gratitude to this person. Picture yourself describing some of your favorite memories. (Pause for reflection.) Now imagine that you are explaining to this person what he has done to make your life better. What have you learned? What has he taught you? How are you in a better place because of him? (Pause for reflection.) Now, if there were some final things you would want to say to this person before you part ways, what would you say?

2. Draft the letter. After students visualize for a while, have them immediately begin writing a letter. Provide these instructions:

> At the top, write "Dear [person's name]," and then write nonstop for the next 10 minutes. Use these sentence stems if you get stuck:
>
> - I remember when _____.
> - I want to thank you for _____.
> - You might not realize how _____.
> - I will never forget _____.
> - You have helped me _____.
> - Because of you, I _____.
> - I want you to know that _____.

3. Show an example video (optional). After students write, I usually show them a video from SoulPancake, a digital entertainment company. The volunteers featured in the video write about people who have positively influenced them and then call to share their feelings. View *An Experiment in Gratitude: The Science of Happiness* (https://www.youtube.com/watch?v=oHv6vTKD6lg). Preview it to see if it's appropriate for your students.

4. Introduce the share. Challenge students to share their letter with their chosen person in some way. I offer three different ways to share:

- **Get it into the person's hands**. You don't have to read the letter to the person, but make sure he gets a chance to read it. It's best if you provide the person with a copy of the letter so he can keep it and reread it.
- **Call the person.** If geography or time is an issue, call the person and read him the letter.
- **Visit the person.** Sitting down to read the letter aloud to the person provides the biggest boost to the happiness of both the reader and the recipient. But it can be challenging. I encourage you to step into the discomfort to get the most authentic experience of gratitude.

5. Report back. Set a challenge deadline for students to share their letter. I usually split my class into groups and have them share their process and experience. Otherwise, ask for students to either write a reflection of the experience or share examples with the full class.

Interconnectedness Web

1. Review the second component of gratitude: recognizing that the source of good lies at least partially beyond ourselves.

2. Have students consider the shirt or a piece of clothing they are wearing. Ask, "Who is someone else who helped bring that shirt into your life?"

As students share ideas, model writing them on the board (I use a concept-web approach). Challenge them—independently, in pairs, or in groups—to come up with at least 12 different people who helped them get that shirt. Guide them to consider different possibilities, such as these:

- The truck driver who transported the shirt
- The farmer who provided the raw material
- The textile engineer

3. Moderate a Discussion. Have students discuss how this brief reflection might influence someone's sense of gratitude. I tell students that, in the future, although they might not pause to physically write another interconnectedness web, they can occasionally take time to think about a few people who contributed to the things they take for granted.

Gratitude Journals and Challenges

Discuss the basic idea of a gratitude journal: finding time in our day to write down good things. I model the basic gratitude reflection with the following stem: '

I am thankful for _____ because _____.

I encourage students to elaborate on the "because" part and, if they are thankful for an experience or an object, to recognize the individual(s) who brought that good thing into their world.

Use journals. Ask students to write about gratitude in their journals, using the following prompts if needed:

- Identify challenges or adversities you've overcome in the past and explain how they've made you a better person.
- Identify people who have taught you important life lessons.

- Identify specific experiences you've had.
- Identify things that make your life more convenient.
- Identify teachers, coaches, or mentors who have helped you.
- Identify positive experiences you've had with people you consider family.
- Identify three of your greatest qualities or strengths and explain why you're grateful to have these qualities and how you could use each in the next week to make the world a better place.

Engage in a social media boost. Challenge students to post, tag, or direct-message an expression of gratitude to someone on social media before the day is over.

Share aloud. Have students volunteer to share good things at the start of each class.

Keep a good things jar. Have students write down a "good thing of the day" on a slip of paper and place it in a large jar or container in the classroom. Pull some occasionally to read aloud.

Draft gratitude notes. Have students write gratitude notes or "shout-outs" for their peers. Have them submit these, review them for appropriateness, and hand them out to recipients (or read the "shout-outs" aloud).

Appendix B:
Making Connections with
a Common Ground Survey

Student's Name: _____ Teacher's Name: _____

10 Things About Me	**10 Things About My Teacher**
1.	1.
2.	2.
3.	3.
4.	4.
5.	5.
6.	6.
7.	7.
8.	8.
9.	9.
10.	10.

Draw a line connecting some of the commonalities. Explain some of the connections you made. What do you and your teacher have in common?

Appendix C:
75 Altruistic Acts
for Educators

1. Plant a tree at school.
2. Call a parent to compliment his child.
3. Give a compliment about a coworker to your boss.
4. Buy dessert for the table near you.
5. Ask a new teacher what you can do to help today.
6. Thank a custodian.
7. Clean something that someone else usually cleans.
8. Post a positive message about someone on social media.
9. Host a drive to collect recyclable cans and donate the money to a local cause.
10. Buy donuts for your colleagues.
11. Leave someone the biggest tip you can afford.
12. Send an e-mail message to a former student to express your pride in her.
13. Invite a new staff member into your conversation.
14. Write a list of things that you love about your partner—and share it.
15. Buy the meal or beverage for the person behind you in line.
16. Use dry erase markers to write affirmations on the bathroom mirror.
17. Smile and say hello to a stranger.
18. Babysit someone's child (or pet) for free.
19. Donate your extra "stuff" using a social media site, local bulletin board, or favorite charity.
20. Call a family member just because (or to express why you appreciate him).
21. Let someone behind you jump ahead in the grocery line.

22. Send anonymous flowers to someone at school.
23. Make a crockpot meal to share in the staff lounge.
24. Recommend a good book.
25. Write a thank-you letter to one of your former teachers or mentors.
26. Donate those clothes you've never worn.
27. Put your phone out of sight and be present in a conversation.
28. Pay off a student's lunch debt anonymously.
29. Ask a substitute teacher what you can do to help her today.
30. Cover a colleague's class when he is out unexpectedly.
31. Compliment your boss.
32. Put an anonymous affirmation on a student's locker or desk.
33. Pay the toll, bus, or train fare for the person behind you.
34. Make dinner for someone who is having a busy week (or phase of life).
35. Clean up litter around your school or in your community.
36. Attend a student's athletic event, hobby-related event, or performance.
37. Return someone else's grocery cart.
38. Put a few dollars in an envelope and write, "If you need this, keep it; otherwise, add to it and pass it on."
39. Tell a student why you're grateful to have her in your class and school.
40. Volunteer at a local soup kitchen. (Bonus points if you get students or coworkers to join you.)
41. Register as a bone marrow donor.
42. Leave a student's favorite treat on his desk before class starts.
43. Repost a friend's, coworker's, or student's blog post.
44. Give a high five to everyone on your way to class.
45. Buy a unique, cool sticker for someone.
46. Write an affirmation on a colleague's board before she gets to work.
47. Let your colleague go ahead of you in the photocopier line.
48. Offer to help a colleague grade papers.
49. Ask your boss what you can do to help her today.

50. Leave extra change in the vending machine.
51. Apologize to someone you wronged.
52. Donate a personal day to a coworker who has a medical need.
53. Volunteer for recess, lunch, or bus duty.
54. Offer to buy a student's art project.
55. Buy a book for a student or colleague.
56. Place a thank-you note in a colleague's mailbox.
57. Invite a student to eat lunch with you.
58. Buy or give a new teacher supplies—especially those you forgot as a new teacher.
59. Help someone carry heavy bags.
60. Organize a DonorsChoose.org project for a colleague.
61. Donate blood (bonus points if you get someone to join you).
62. Post online something you love about your school.
63. Mix up a big batch of hot chocolate to give out to strangers or students on a cold day (or lemonade on a hot day).
64. Write a recommendation letter for a student without being asked.
65. Pull a student aside to tell him how much you've noticed a positive character trait, such as resilience.
66. Call a friend you haven't talked to in a long time.
67. Leave a thank-you note or gift card for your mail carrier.
68. Put an anonymous affirmation in a colleague's mailbox.
69. Restock the staff coffee bar with the best stuff you can afford.
70. Clean out the refrigerator in the staff lounge.
71. Have your students come up with a "prospiracy" for a colleague (see Chapter 8).
72. Post a good review online for a business you frequent.
73. Have your restaurant server box up half your meal in advance and then give it away to someone in need.
74. Clean the snow and ice off someone else's car.
75. Send a care package to someone serving overseas.

Appendix D: Resources for Positive Psychology

Among the many resources in the booming field of positive psychology, the ones listed here have been foundational to my understanding of the science of well-being and related practical strategies. I hope these boost your personal and professional well-being as much as they've boosted mine!

Websites
- The Greater Good (University of California, Berkeley) www.greatergood.berkeley.edu
- Positive Psychology Center (University of Pennsylvania) ppc.sas.upenn.edu

Books by Topic
Understanding Positive Psychology Theories
- *Activities for Teaching Positive Psychology: A Guide for Instructors,* by Jeffrey Froh and Acacia Parks
- *Authentic Happiness: Using the New Positive Psychology to Realize Your Potential for Lasting Fulfillment,* by Martin Seligman
- *The Compassionate Instinct: The Science of Human Goodness,* edited by Dacher Keltner, Jason Marsh, and Jeremy Adam Smith
- *Flourish: A Visionary New Understanding of Happiness and Well-being,* by Martin Seligman

- *Happier: Learn the Secrets to Daily Joy and Lasting Fulfillment,* by Tal Ben-Shahar
- *The Happiness Advantage: How a Positive Brain Fuels Success in Work and Life,* by Shawn Achor
- *The How of Happiness: A Scientific Approach to Getting the Life You Want,* by Sonja Lyubomirsky
- *The Myths of Happiness: What Should Make You Happy but Doesn't, What Shouldn't Make You Happy but Does,* by Sonja Lyubomirsky
- *A Primer in Positive Psychology,* by Christopher Peterson

Understanding Optimism

- *Learned Optimism: How to Change Your Mind and Your Life,* by Martin Seligman

Understanding Accomplishment and Goal Striving

- *Flow: The Psychology of Optimal Experience,* by Mihaly Csikszentmihalyi
- *Grit: The Power of Passion and Perseverance,* by Angela Duckworth
- *The Power of Habit: Why We Do What We Do in Life and Business,* by Charles Duhigg
- *Rethinking Positive Thinking: Inside the New Science of Motivation,* by Gabriele Oettingen
- *Why We Do What We Do: Understanding Self-motivation,* by Edward Deci

Understanding Human Connection

- *Connected: The Surprising Power of Our Social Networks and How They Shape Our Lives,* by Nicholas A. Christakis and James H. Fowler
- *Empathy: Why It Matters and How to Get It,* by Roman Krznaric

Understanding Mindfulness

- *Focus: The Hidden Driver of Excellence,* by Daniel Goleman
- *The Mindful Way Through Depression: Freeing Yourself from Chronic Unhappiness,* by Mark Williams, John Teasdale, Zindel Segal, and Jon Kabat-Zinn
- *The Miracle of Mindfulness: An Introduction to the Practice of Meditation,* by Thich Nhat Hanh (author) and Vo-Dihn Mai (illustrator)
- *Teach, Breathe, Learn: Mindfulness in and out of the Classroom,* by Meena Srinivasan
- *10% Happier: How I Tamed the Voice in My Head, Reduced Stress Without Losing My Edge, and Found Self-Help That Actually Works,* by Dan Harris

Understanding Gratitude

- *Thanks! How Practicing Gratitude Can Make You Happier,* by Robert Emmons

References

Abramson, L. Y., Seligman, M. E., & Teasdale, J. D. (1978). Learned help-lessness in humans: Critique and reformulation. *Journal of Abnormal Psychology, 87*(1), 49–74. doi:10.1037//0021-843x.87.1.49

Aknin, L. B., Barrington-Leigh, C. P., Dunn, E. W., Helliwell, J. F., Burns, J., Biswas-Diener, R., et al. (2013). Prosocial spending and well-being: Cross-cultural evidence for a psychological universal. *Journal of Personality and Social Psychology, 104*(4), 635–652.

Albertson, E. R., Neff, K. D., & Dill-Shackleford, K. E. (2014). Self-compassion and body dissatisfaction in women: A randomized controlled trial of a brief meditation intervention. *Mindfulness, 6*(3), 444–454. doi:10.1007/s12671-014-0277-3

Appel, H., Gerlach, A. L., & Crusius, J. (2016). The interplay between Facebook use, social comparison, envy, and depression. *Current Opinion in Psychology, 9*, 44–49. doi:10.1016/j.copsyc.2015.10.006

Aron, A., Melinat, E., Aron, E. N., Vallone, R. D., & Bator, R. J. (1997). The experimental generation of interpersonal closeness: A procedure and some preliminary findings. *Personality and Social Psychology Bulletin, 23*(4), 363–377. doi:10.1177/0146167297234003

Barnes, S., Brown, K. W., Krusemark, E., Campbell, W. K., & Rogge, R. D. (2007). The role of mindfulness in romantic relationship satisfaction and responses to relationship stress. *Journal of Marital and Family Therapy, 33*(4), 482–500. doi:10.1111/j.1752-0606.2007.00033.x

Bartlett, M. Y., & DeSteno, D. (2006). Gratitude and prosocial behavior. *Psychological Science, 17*(4), 319–325. doi:10.1111/j.1467-9280.2006.01705.x

Berg, J. M., Dutton, J. E., & Wrzesniewski, A. (2007). What is job crafting and why does it matter? Ann Arbor, MI: Center for Positive Organizational Scholarship. Regents of the University of Michigan.

Berg, J. M., Dutton, J. E., & Wrzesniewski, A. (2013). Job crafting and meaningful work. In B. J. Dik, Z. S. Byrne, & M. F. Steger (Eds.), *Purpose and meaning in the workplace* (pp. 81–104). Washington, DC: American Psychological Association.

Bertini, E. (2017, June 15). Can visualization elicit empathy? Our experiments with "anthropographics." *Medium*. Retrieved April 3, 2018, from https://medium.com/@FILWD/can-visualization-elicit-empathy-our-experiments-with-anthropographics-7e13590be204

Bianchi, R., & Schonfeld, I. S. (2016). Burnout is associated with a depressive cognitive style. *Personality and Individual Differences, 100*, 1–5. doi:10.1016/j.paid.2016.01.008

Bloom, P. (2017, February 19). Think empathy makes the world a better place? Think again. *The Guardian*. Retrieved March 24, 2018, from https://www.theguardian.com/commentisfree/2017/feb/19/think-empathy-makes-world-better-place-think-again

Bridge, D. J., & Paller, K. A. (2012). Neural correlates of reactivation and retrieval-induced distortion. *Journal of Neuroscience, 32*(35), 12144–12151. doi:10.1523/jneurosci.1378-12.2012

Bridge, D. J., & Voss, J. L. (2014). Hippocampal binding of novel information with dominant memory traces can support both memory stability and change. *Journal of Neuroscience, 34*(6), 2203–2213. doi:10.1523/jneurosci.3819-13.2014

Brown, B. (Speaker). (2013, August 15). *The power of vulnerability: Brené Brown* [Video]. London: The RSA. Retrieved March 24, 2018, from https://www.youtube.com/watch?v=sXSjc-pbXk4

Brunstein, J. C., Schultheiss, O. C., & Grässman, R. (1998). Personal goals and emotional well-being: The moderating role of motive dispositions. *Journal of Personality and Social Psychology, 75*, 494–508.

Buchanan, K. E., & Bardi, A. (2010). Acts of kindness and acts of novelty affect life satisfaction. *Journal of Social Psychology, 150*(3), 235–237. doi:10.1080/00224540903365554

Butler, A. C., Chapman, J. E., Forman, E. M., & Beck, A. T. (2006). The empirical status of cognitive-behavioral therapy: A review of meta-analyses. *Clinical Psychology Review, 26*(1), 17–31. doi:10.1016/j.cpr.2005.07.003

Caprariello, P. A., & Reis, H. T. (2013). To do, to have, or to share: Valuing of experiences over material possessions depends on the involvement of others. *Journal of Personality and Social Psychology, 104*, 199–215. http://dx.doi.org/10.1037/a0030953

Carlsmith, K. M., Wilson, T. D., & Gilbert, D. T. (2008). The paradoxical consequences of revenge. *Journal of Personality and Social Psychology, 95*(6), 1316–1324. doi:10.1037/a0012165

Carlson, L. E., & Garland, S. N. (2005). Impact of mindfulness-based stress reduction (MBSR) on sleep, mood, stress and fatigue symptoms in cancer outpatients. *International Journal of Behavioral Medicine, 12*(4), 278–285. doi:10.1207/s15327558ijbm1204_9

Center for Positive Organizations. (2018). Job Crafting™ Exercise. Ann Arbor, MI: Author. Retrieved February 16, 2018, from http://positiveorgs.bus.umich.edu/cpo-tools/job-crafting-exercise/

Chan, D. W. (2011). Burnout and life satisfaction: Does gratitude intervention make a difference among Chinese school teachers in Hong Kong? *Educational Psychology, 31*(7), 809–823. doi:10.1080/01443410.2011.608525

Christakis, N. A., & Fowler, J. H. (2011). *Connected: The surprising power of our social networks and how they shape our lives: How your friends' friends' friends affect everything you feel, think, and do.* New York: Back Bay Books.

Clark, A. E., Diener, E., Georgellis, Y., & Lucas, R. E. (2003). *Lags and leads in life satisfaction: A test of the baseline hypothesis.* Berlin: DIW.

Cohen, A. (2004, October 1). Research on the science of forgiveness: An annotated bibliography. *Greater Good Magazine.* Retrieved January 9, 2018, from https://greatergood.berkeley.edu/article/item/the_science_of_forgiveness_an_annotated_bibliography

Corr, P. J., & Gray, J. A. (1995). Attributional style, socialization and cognitive ability as predictors of sales success: A predictive validity study. *Personality and Individual Differences, 18*(2), 241–252. doi:10.1016/0191-8869(94)00153-j

Csikszentmihalyi, M. (2009). *Flow: The psychology of optimal experience.* New York: Harper Row.

Danese, A., & McEwen, B. S. (2012). Adverse childhood experiences, allostasis, allostatic load, and age-related disease. *Physiology & Behavior, 106*(1), 29–39. doi:10.1016/j.physbeh.2011.08.019

Davies, S. (2011). The effect of mindfulness-based therapy on anxiety and depression: A meta-analytic review. *Primary Health Care, 21*(3), 14–14. doi:10.7748/phc.21.3.14.s12

Diener, E. (2000). Subjective well-being: The science of happiness and a proposal for a national index. *American Psychologist, 55*(1), 34–43. doi:10.1037//0003-066x.55.1.34

Diener, E., Lucas, R. E., & Scollon, C. N. (2009). Beyond the hedonic treadmill: Revising the adaptation theory of well-being. In E. Diener (Ed.), *The science of well-being* (pp. 103–118). Dordrecht, Netherlands: Springer. doi:10.1007/978-90-481-2350-6_5

Diener, E., Sandvik, E., & Pavot, W. (2009). Happiness is the frequency, not the intensity, of positive versus negative affect. In E. Diener (Ed.), *The science of well-being* (pp. 213–231). Dordrecht, Netherlands: Springer doi:10.1007/978-90-481-2354-4_10

Dijkstra, M. T., Beersma, B., & Evers, A. (2011). Reducing conflict-related employee strain: The benefits of an internal locus of control and a problem-solving conflict management strategy. *Work & Stress, 25*(2), 167–184.

Dittrich, L. (2017). *Patient H. M.: A story of memory, madness, and family secrets.* London: Vintage.

Doidge, N. (2017). *The brain that changes itself: Stories of personal triumph from the frontiers of brain science.* New York: Penguin.

Drew, T., Võ, M. L. H., & Wolfe, J. M. (2013). The invisible gorilla strikes again. *Psychological Science, 24*(9), 1848–1853. doi:10.1177/0956797613479386

Dunn, E. W., Aknin, L. B., & Norton, M. I. (2014). Prosocial spending and happiness. *Current Directions in Psychological Science, 23*(1), 41–47. doi:10.1177/0963721413512503

Durant, W. (1991). *The story of philosophy: The lives and opinions of the world's greatest philosophers.* New York: Pocket Books.

Elliot, A. J., & Sheldon, K. M. (1998). Avoidance personal goals and the personality–illness relationship. *Journal of Personality and Social Psychology, 75*, 1282–1299.

Emmons, R. A. (1986). Personal strivings: An approach to personality and subjective well-being. *Journal of Personality and Social Psychology, 51*, 1058–1068.

Emmons, R. A. (1991). Personal strivings, daily life events, and psychological and physical well-being. *Journal of Personality, 59*, 453–472.

Emmons, R. A. (1999). *The psychology of ultimate concerns: Motivation and spirituality in personality.* New York: Guilford Press.

Emmons, R. A. (2007). *Thanks! How the new science of gratitude can make you happier.* Boston: Houghton Mifflin.

Forgeard, M. J. C., & Seligman, M. E. P. (2012). Seeing the glass half full: A review of the causes and consequences of optimism. *Pratiques Psychologiques, 18*(2), 107–120. doi:10.1016/j.prps.2012.02.002

Fowler, J. H., & Christakis, N. A. (2010). Cooperative behavior cascades in human social networks. *Proceedings of the National Academy of Sciences, 107*(12), 5334–5338. doi:10.1073/pnas.0913149107

Gable, S. L., Reis, H. T., Impett, E. A., & Asher, E. R. (2004). What do you do when things go right? The intrapersonal and interpersonal benefits of sharing positive events. *Journal of Personality and Social Psychology, 87*(2), 228–245. doi:10.1037/0022-3514.87.2.228

Gehlbach, H., Brinkworth, M. E., King, A. M., Hsu, L., McIntyre, J., & Rogers, T. (2016). Creating birds of similar feathers: Leveraging similarity to improve teacher-student relationships and academic achievement. *Journal of Educational Psychology, 108*(3), 342–352.

Gladstone, T. R., & Kaslow, N. J. (1995). Depression and attributions in children and adolescents: A meta-analytic review. *Journal of Abnormal Child Psychology, 23*(5), 597–606. doi:10.1007/bf01447664

Goleman, D. (2008, March 1). Hot to help: When can empathy move us to action? *Greater Good Magazine.* Retrieved March 24, 2018, from https://greatergood.berkeley.edu/article/item/hot_to_help

Gordon, R. A. (2008). Attributional style and athletic performance: Strategic optimism and defensive pessimism. *Psychology of Sport and Exercise, 9*(3), 336–350. doi:10.1016/j.psychsport.2007.04.007

Gottman, J. (Speaker). (2012, April 18). *Four negative patterns that predict divorce* [Video]. Retrieved April 4, 2018, from https://www.youtube.com/watch?v=625t8Rr9o6o

Grant, A. M. (2007). Relational job design and the motivation to make a prosocial difference. *Academy of Management Review, 32*(2), 393–417. doi:10.5465/amr.2007.24351328

Greater Good in Action. (n.d.). Putting a human face on suffering. Retrieved April 3, 2018, from https://ggia.berkeley.edu/practice/putting_a_human_face_on_suffering

Greidanus, E., & Everall, R. D. (2010). Helper therapy in an online suicide prevention community. *British Journal of Guidance & Counselling, 38*(2), 191–204. doi:10.1080/03069881003600991

Hajdu, T., & Hajdu, G. (2017). The association between experiential and material expenditures and subjective well-being: New evidence from Hungarian survey data. *Journal of Economic Psychology, 62*, 72–86. doi:10.1016/j.joep.2017.06.009

Hanh, T. (1975). *The miracle of mindfulness: An introduction to the practice of meditation.* Boston: Beacon Press.

Hanson, R. (2015, June 25). Just one thing: Forgive yourself. *Greater Good Magazine.* Retrieved January 9, 2018, from https://greatergood.berkeley.edu/article/item/just_one_thing_forgive_yourself

Harbaugh, W. T., Mayr, U., & Burghart, D. R. (2007). Neural responses to taxation and voluntary giving reveal motives for charitable donations. *Science, 316*(5831), 1622–1625. doi:10.1126/science.1140738

Harris, A. H, Luskin, F., Norman, S. B., Standard, S., Bruning, J., Evans, S., & Thoresen, C. E. (2006). Effects of a group forgiveness intervention on forgiveness, perceived stress and trait anger: A randomized trial. *Journal of Clinical Psychology, 62*(6) 715–733.

Hasenkamp, W., Wilson-Mendenhall, C. D., Duncan, E., & Barsalou, L. W. (2012). Mind wandering and attention during focused meditation: A fine-grained temporal analysis of fluctuating cognitive states. *Neuro-Image, 59*(1), 750–760. doi:10.1016/j.neuroimage.2011.07.008

Hattie, J. (2012). *Visible learning for teachers maximizing impact on learning.* London: Routledge.

Hersher, R. (2017, June 1). The making of emotions, from pleasurable fear to bittersweet relief. NPR. Retrieved April 6, 2018, from https://www.npr.org/sections/health-shots/2017/06/01/530103479/the-making-of-emotions-from-pleasurable-fear-to-bittersweet-relief

Hölzel, B. K., Carmody, J., Vangel, M., Congleton, C., Yerramsetti, S. M., Gard, T., & Lazar, S. W. (2011). Mindfulness practice leads to increases in regional brain gray matter density. *Psychiatry Research: Neuroimaging, 191*(1), 36–43. doi:10.1016/j.pscychresns.2010.08.006

Hunter, J. C. (2012). *The servant: A simple story about the true essence of leadership.* New York: Crown Business.

Hyman, I. E., Boss, S. M., Wise, B. M., McKenzie, K. E., & Caggiano, J. M. (2010). Did you see the unicycling clown? Inattentional blindness while walking and talking on a cell phone. *Applied Cognitive Psychology, 24*(5), 597–607. doi:10.1002/acp.1638

Ingersoll, R. M. (2012, May 16). Beginning teacher induction: What the data tell us: Induction is an education reform whose time has come. *Education Week.* Retrieved from http://www.edweek.org/ew/articles/2012/05/16/kappan_ingersoll.h31.html?tkn=M

Ingersoll, R. M., Merrill, L., & Stuckey, D. (2014). Seven trends: The transformation of the teaching force, updated April 2014. *CPRE Report* (No.RR-80). Philadelphia: Consortium for Policy Research in Education, University of Pennsylvania.

Jennings, P. A., Brown, J. L., Frank, J. L., Doyle, S., Oh, Y., Davis, R., et al. (2017). Impacts of the CARE for Teachers program on teachers' social and emotional competence and classroom interactions. *Journal of Educational Psychology, 109*(7), 1010–1028.

Jerath, R. (2006). Physiology of long pranayamic breathing: Neural respiratory elements may provide a mechanism that explains how slow deep breathing shifts the autonomic nervous system. *Journal of Yoga & Physical Therapy, 67*(3), 566–571. doi:10.4172/2157-7595.1000252

Jones, D. (2015, January 9). The 36 questions that lead to love. *The New York Times.* Retrieved January 2, 2018, from https://www.nytimes.com/2015/01/11/fashion/no-37-big-wedding-or-small.html

Judge, T. A., & Bono, J. E. (2001). Relationship of core self-evaluations traits—self-esteem, generalized self-efficacy, locus of control, and emotional stability—with job satisfaction and job performance: A meta-analysis. *Journal of Applied Psychology, 86*(1), 80–92.

Judge, T. A., Bono, J. E., Erez, A., & Locke, E. A. (2005). Core self-evaluations and job and life satisfaction: The role of self-concordance and goal attainment. *Journal of Applied Psychology, 90*(2), 257–268. doi:10.1037/0021-9010.90.2.257

Kahneman, D. (2010). *The riddle of experience vs. memory* [Video]. TED. Retrieved April 6, 2018, from https://www.ted.com/talks /daniel_kahneman_the_riddle_of_experience_vs_memory/

Karremans, J. C., & Van Lange, P. A. M. (2005). Does activating justice help or hurt in promoting forgiveness? *Journal of Experimental Social Psychology, 41*(3), 290–297. doi:10.1016/j.jesp.2004.06.005

Kasser, T., & Ryan, R. M. (1996). Further examining the American dream: Differential correlates of intrinsic and extrinsic goals. *Personality and Social Psychology Bulletin, 22,* 280–287.

Killingsworth, M. (2013, July 16). Does mind-wandering make you unhappy? *Greater Good Magazine.* Retrieved January 2, 2018, from https://greatergood.berkeley.edu/article/item/does_mind _wandering_make_you_unhappy

King, L. A., & Emmons, R. A. (1991). Psychological, physical, and interpersonal correlates of emotional expressiveness, conflict, and control. *European Journal of Personality, 5,* 131–150.

Klinger, E. (1998). The search for meaning in evolutionary perspective and its clinical implications. In P. T. P. Wong & P. S. Fry (Eds.), *Handbook of personal meaning: Theory, research, and application* (pp. 27–50). Mahwah, NJ: Erlbaum.

Klug, H. J., & Maier, G. W. (2014). Linking goal progress and subjective well-being: A meta-analysis. *Journal of Happiness Studies, 16*(1), 37–65. doi:10.1007/s10902-013-9493-0

Koo, M., Algoe, S. B., Wilson, T. D., & Gilbert, D. T. (2008). It's a wonderful life: Mentally subtracting positive events improves people's affective states, contrary to their affective forecasts. *Journal of Personality and Social Psychology, 95*(5), 1217–1224. doi:10.1037/a0013316

Kuhbandner, C., Pekrun, R., & Maier, M. A. (2010). The role of positive and negative affect in the "mirroring" of other persons' actions. *Cognition and Emotion, 24*(7), 1182–1190.

Kumar, A., Killingsworth, M. A., & Gilovich, T. D. (2014). Waiting for Merlot: Anticipatory consumption of experiential and material purchases. *Psychological Science, 25*(10), 1924–1931. doi:10.1037 /e573552014-098

Lambert, N. M., Clark, M. S., Durtschi, J., Fincham, F. D., & Graham, S. M. (2010). Benefits of expressing gratitude. *Psychological Science, 21*(4), 574–580. doi:10.1177/0956797610364003

Layous, K., Nelson, S. K., Kurtz, J. L., & Lyubomirsky, S. (2016). What triggers prosocial effort? A positive feedback loop between positive activities, kindness, and well-being. *The Journal of Positive Psychology, 12*(4), 385–398. doi:10.1080/17439760.2016.1198924

Lehrer, J. (2012, February 28). The paradox of altruism. *Wired*. Retrieved June 3, 2017, from www.wired.com/2012/02/the-paradox-of-altruism/

Levy, L., Howard, T., & Aronczyk, A. (2018, January 9). How to be a hero [Audio blog post]. WNYC Studios. Retrieved from http://www.radiolab.org/story/how-be-hero/

Li, X., Meng, X., Li, H., Yang, J., & Yuan, J. (2017). The impact of mood on empathy for pain: Evidence from an EEG study. *Psychophysiology, 54*(9), 1311–1322. doi:10.1111/psyp.12882

Likowski, K. U., Weyers, P., Seibt, B., Stöhr, C., Pauli, P., & Mühlberger, A. (2011). Sad and lonely? Sad mood suppresses facial mimicry. *Journal of Nonverbal Behavior, 35*(2), 101–117. doi:10.1007/s10919-011-0107-4

Locke, E. A., & Latham, G. P. (2006). New directions in goal-setting theory. *Current Directions in Psychological Science, 15*(5), 265–268. doi:10.1111/j.1467-8721.2006.00449.x

Lyubomirsky, S., & Della Porta, M. (2012). Boosting happiness, buttressing resilience: Results from cognitive and behavioral interventions. In J. W. Reich, A. J. Zautra, & J. Hall (Eds.), *Handbook of adult resilience: Concepts, methods, and applications* (pp. 450–464). New York: Guilford Press.

Lyubomirsky, S., & Nolen-Hoeksema, S. (1995). Effects of self-focused rumination on negative thinking and interpersonal problem solving. *Journal of Personality and Social Psychology, 69*(1), 176–190. doi:10.1037//0022-3514.69.1.176

MacLeod, A. K., Coates, E., & Hetherton, J. (2007). Increasing well-being through teaching goal-setting and planning skills: Results of a brief intervention. *Journal of Happiness Studies, 9*(2), 185–196. doi:10.1007/s10902-007-9057-2

Manns, J. R., & Bass, D. I. (2016). The amygdala and prioritization of declarative memories. *Current Directions in Psychological Science, 25*(4), 261–265. doi:10.1177/0963721416654456

Martela, F., & Ryan, R. M. (2016). Prosocial behavior increases well-being and vitality even without contact with the beneficiary: Causal and behavioral evidence. *Motivation and Emotion, 40*(3), 351–357. doi:10.1007/s11031-016-9552-z

Martin-Krumm, C. P., Sarrazin, P. G., Peterson, C., & Famose, J-P. (2003). Explanatory style and resilience after sports failure. *Personality and Individual Differences, 35*(7), 1685–1695. doi:10.1016/s0191-8869(02)00390-2

McAdams, D. P., de St. Aubin, E., & Logan, R. L. (1993). Generativity among young, midlife, and older adults. *Psychology and Aging, 8,* 221–230.

McCullough, M. E., & Witvliet, C. V. (2001). The psychology of forgiveness. In C. R. Snyder & S. J. Lopez (Eds.), *Handbook of positive psychology* (pp. 446-458). Oxford: Oxford University Press.

McGreevey, S. (2011, April 22). Turn down the volume. *Harvard Gazette.* Retrieved January 2, 2018, from https://news.harvard.edu/gazette/story/2011/04/turn-down-the-volume/

Medina, J. (2014). *Brain rules: 12 principles for surviving and thriving at work, home, and school.* Seattle: Pear Press.

Mehl, M. R., Vazire, S., Holleran, S. E., & Clark, C. S. (2010). Eavesdropping on happiness: Well-being is related to having less small talk and more substantive conversations. *Psychological Science, 21*(4), 539–541. http://doi.org/10.1177/0956797610362675

Miller, J. C., & Krizan, Z. (2016). Walking facilitates positive affect (even when expecting the opposite). *Emotion, 16*(5), 775–785. doi:10.1037/a0040270

Mills, P. J., Redwine, L., Wilson, K., Pung, M. A., Chinh, K., Greenberg, B. H., et al. (2015). The role of gratitude in spiritual well-being in asymptomatic heart failure patients. *Spirituality in Clinical Practice, 2*(1), 5–17. doi:10.1037/scp0000050

Moser, J. S., Dougherty, A., Mattson, W. I., Katz, B., Moran, T. P., Guevarra, D., et al. (2017). Third-person self-talk facilitates emotion regulation without engaging cognitive control: Converging evidence from ERP and fMRI. *Scientific Reports, 7*(1), 4519. doi:10.1038/s41598-017-04047-3

Musick, M. A., & Wilson, J. (2003). Volunteering and depression: The role of psychological and social resources in different age groups. *Social Science & Medicine, 56*(2), 259–269. doi:10.1016/s0277-9536(02)00025-4

Nelson-Coffey, S. K., Fritz, M. M., Lyubomirsky, S., & Cole, S. W. (2017). Kindness in the blood: A randomized controlled trial of the gene regulatory impact of prosocial behavior. *Psychoneuroendocrinology, 81,* 8–13. doi:10.1016/j.psyneuen.2017.03.025

Nelson-Coffey, S. K., Layous, K., Cole, S. W., & Lyubomirsky, S. (2016). Do unto others or treat yourself? The effects of prosocial and self-focused behavior on psychological flourishing. *Emotion, 16*(6), 850–861.

Newman, K. (2017, July 25). How the science of well-being is evolving. *Greater Good Magazine.* Retrieved January 3, 2018, from https://greatergood.berkeley.edu/article/item/how_the_science_of_well_being_is_evolving

Oettingen, G. (2015). *Rethinking positive thinking: Inside the new science of motivation.* New York: Current.

Okonofua, J. A., Paunesku, D., & Walton, G. M. (2016). Brief intervention to encourage empathic discipline cuts suspension rates in half among adolescents. *Proceedings of the National Academy of Sciences, 113*(19), 5221–5226. doi:10.1073/pnas.1523698113

One man's life of no regrets. (1972, March 24). *Life, 66*–68.

Ong, A. D., Benson, L., Zautra, A. J., & Ram, N. (2018). Emodiversity and biomarkers of inflammation. *Emotion, 18*(1), 3–14. doi:10.1037/emo0000343

Parkay, F. W., Greenwood, G., Olejnik, S., & Proller, N. (1988). A study of the relationships among teacher efficacy, locus of control, and stress. *Journal of Research & Development in Education, 21*(4), 13–22.

Pelucchi, S., Paleari, F. G., Regalia, C., & Fincham, F. D. (2015). Self-forgiveness in romantic relationships: 2. Impact on interpersonal forgiveness. *Family Science, 6*(1), 181–190. doi:10.1080/19424620.2015.1082048

Peterson, C., Seligman, M. E., & Vaillant, G. E. (1988). Pessimistic explanatory style is a risk factor for physical illness: A thirty-five-year longitudinal study. *Journal of Personality and Social Psychology, 55*(1), 23–27. doi:10.1017/cbo9780511759048.018

Rao, S. (2010). *Happiness at work: Be resilient, motivated, and successful— no matter what.* New York: McGraw-Hill.

Raposa, E. B., Laws, H. B., & Ansell, E. B. (2015). Prosocial behavior mitigates the negative effects of stress in everyday life. *Clinical Psychological Science, 4*(4), 691–698.

Rettew, D., & Reivich, K. (1995). Sports and explanatory style. In G. M. Buchanan & M. E. P. Seligman (Eds.), *Explanatory style* (pp. 173–185). Hillsdale, NJ: Erlbaum.

Roeser, R. W., Schonert-Reichl, K. A., Jha, A., Cullen, M., Wallace, L., Wilensky, R., et al. (2013). Mindfulness training and reductions in teacher stress and burnout: Results from two randomized, waitlist-control field trials. *Journal of Educational Psychology, 105*(3), 787–804. doi:10.1037/a0032093

Rudd, M., Aaker, J., & Norton, M. I. (2014). Getting the most out of giving: Concretely framing a prosocial goal maximizes happiness. *Journal of Experimental Social Psychology, 54*, 11–24. doi:10.1016/j.jesp.2014.04.002

Ryff, C. D. (1989). Happiness is everything, or is it? Explorations on the meaning of psychological well-being. *Journal of Personality and Social Psychology, 57*, 1069–1081.

Schäfer, T., Sedlmeier, P., Städtler, C., & Huron, D. (2013). The psychological functions of music listening. *Frontiers in Psychology, 4*, 511. doi:10.3389/fpsyg.2013.00511

Schwartz, C., Meisenhelder, J. B., Ma, Y., & Reed, G. (2003). Altruistic social interest behaviors are associated with better mental health. *Psychosomatic Medicine, 65*(5), 778–785. doi:10.1097/01.psy.0000079378.39062.d4

Seligman, M. E. P. (1972). Learned helplessness. *Annual Review of Medicine, 23*(1), 407–412. doi:10.1146/annurev.me.23.020172.002203

Seligman, M. E. P. (2011). *Learned optimism.* North Sydney, NSW: William Heinemann Australia.

Seligman, M. E. P., Castellon, C., Cacciola, J., Schulman, P., Luborsky, L., Oilove, M., & Downing, R. (1988). Explanatory style change during cognitive therapy for unipolar depression. *Journal of Abnormal Psychology, 97*(1), 13–18. doi:10.1037//0021-843x.97.1.13

Seligman, M. E. P., Nolen-Hoeksema, S., Thornton, N., & Thornton, K. M. (1990). Explanatory style as a mechanism of disappointing athletic performance. *Psychological Science, 1*(2), 143–146. doi:10.1111/j.1467-9280.1990.tb00084.x

Seligman, M. E. P., & Schulman, P. (1986). Explanatory style as a predictor of productivity and quitting among life insurance sales agents. *Journal of Personality and Social Psychology, 50*(4), 832–838. doi:10.1037//0022-3514.50.4.832

Seligman, M. E. P., Steen, T. A., Park, N., & Peterson, C. (2005). Positive psychology progress: Empirical validation of interventions. *American Psychologist, 60*(5), 410–421. doi:10.1037/0003-066x.60.5.410

Seligman, M. E. P., & Tierney, J. (2017, May 19). We aren't built to live in the moment. *The New York Times.* Retrieved from https://www.nytimes.com/2017/05/19/opinion/sunday/why-the-future-is-always-on-your-mind.html

Sheldon, K. M., & Elliot, A. J. (1999). Goal striving, need satisfaction, and longitudinal well-being: The self-concordance model.

Journal of Personality and Social Psychology, 76(3), 482–497. doi:10.1037//0022-3514.76.3.482

Sheldon, K. M., & Kasser, T. (1998). Pursuing personal goals: Skills enable progress, but not all progress is beneficial. *Personality & Social Psychology Bulletin, 24,* 1319–1331.

Sheldon, K. M., & Lyubomirsky, S. (2007). Is it possible to become happier? (And if so, how?). *Social and Personality Psychology Compass, 1*(1), 129–145. doi:10.1111/j.1751-9004.2007.00002.x

Silani, G., Lamm, C., Ruff, C. C., & Singer, T. (2013). Right supramarginal gyrus is crucial to overcome emotional egocentricity bias in social judgments. *Journal of Neuroscience, 33*(39), 15466–15476.

Sims, T., Reed, A. E., & Carr, D. C. (2016). Information and communication technology use is related to higher well-being among the oldest-old. *The Journals of Gerontology Series B: Psychological Sciences and Social Sciences, 72*(5), 761–770. doi:10.1093/geronb/gbw130

Singh, J. A., Obyrne, M. M., Colligan, R. C., & Lewallen, D. G. (2010). Pessimistic explanatory style: A psychological risk factor for poor pain and functional outcomes two years after knee replacement. *Journal of Bone and Joint Surgery—British Volume, 92-B*(6), 799–806. doi:10.1302/0301-620x.92b6.23114

Sivers, D. (2010). *Keep your goals to yourself* [Video]. TED. Retrieved from https://www.ted.com/talks/derek_sivers_keep_your_goals_to_yourself

Stanford Center for the Study of Language and Information. (2013, July 21). Biological altruism. *Stanford Encyclopedia of Philosophy.* Stanford, CA: Author. Retrieved from https://plato.stanford.edu/entries/altruism-biological/#ButItReaAlt

Street, H., Nathan, P., Durkin, K., Morling, J., Dzahari, M. A., Carson, J., & Durkin, E. (2004). Understanding the relationships between wellbeing, goal-setting and depression in children. *Australian & New Zealand Journal of Psychiatry, 38*(3), 155–161. doi:10.1080/j.1440-1614.2004.01317.x

Suh, E., Diener, E., & Fujita, F. (1996). Events and subjective well-being: Only recent events matter. *Journal of Personality and Social Psychology, 70*(5), 1091–1102. doi:10.1037//0022-3514.70.5.1091

Suttie, J. (2017, December 4). How a bad mood affects empathy in your brain. *Greater Good Magazine.* Retrieved April 3, 2018, from https://greatergood.berkeley.edu/article/item/how_a_bad_mood_affects_empathy_in_yoUr_brain

Van Noorden, T. H., Haselager, G. J., Cillessen, A. H., & Bukowski, W. M. (2014). Empathy and involvement in bullying in children and adolescents: A systematic review. *Journal of Youth and Adolescence, 44*(3), 637–657. doi:10.1007/s10964-014-0135-6

Varese, F., Smeets, F., Drukker, M., Lieverse, R., Lataster, T., Viechtbauer, W., et al. (2012). Childhood adversities increase the risk of psychosis: A meta-analysis of patient-control, prospective- and cross-sectional cohort studies. *Schizophrenia Bulletin, 38*(4), 661–671. doi:10.1093/schbul/sbs050

Verduyn, P., Ybarra, O., Résibois, M., Jonides, J., & Kross, E. (2017). Do social network sites enhance or undermine subjective well-being? A critical review. *Social Issues and Policy Review, 11*(1), 274–302. doi:10.1111/sipr.12033

Wallace-Hadrill, S. M. A., & Kamboj, S. K. (2016). The impact of perspective change as a cognitive reappraisal strategy on affect: A systematic review. *Frontiers in Psychology, 7*, 1715. http://doi.org/10.3389/fpsyg.2016.01715

Watson, H., Rapee, R., & Todorov, N. (2015). Imagery rescripting of revenge, avoidance, and forgiveness for past bullying experiences in young adults. *Cognitive Behaviour Therapy, 45*(1), 73–89. doi:10.1080/16506073.2015.1108360

Weick, K. (1986). Small wins. *Redefining Social Problems*, 29–48. doi:10.1007/978-1-4899-2236-6_3

Wiese, B. S., & Freund, A. M. (2005). Goal progress makes one happy, or does it? Longitudinal findings from the work domain. *Journal of Occupational and Organizational Psychology, 78*, 1–19.

Williams, M., Teasdale, J., Segal, Z., & Kabat-Zinn, J. (2007). *The mindful way through depression: Freeing yourself from chronic unhappiness.* New York: Guilford Press.

Wiseman, T. (1996). A concept analysis of empathy. *Journal of Advanced Nursing, 23*(6), 1162–1167. doi:10.1046/j.1365-2648.1996.12213.x

Witvliet, C. V., DeYoung, N. J., Hofelich, A. J., & DeYoung, P. A. (2011). Compassionate reappraisal and emotion suppression as alternatives to offense-focused rumination: Implications for forgiveness and psychophysiological well-being. *The Journal of Positive Psychology, 6*(4), 286–299. doi:10.1080/17439760.2011.577091

Witvliet, C. V., Ludwig, T. E., & Vander Laan, K. L. (2001). Granting forgiveness or harboring grudges: Implications for emotion, physiology, and health. *Psychological Science, 12*(2), 117–123. doi:10.1111/1467-9280.00320

Witvliet, C. V., Worthington, E. L., Jr., Root, L. M., Sato, A. F., Ludwig, T. E., & Exline, J. J. (2008). Retributive justice, restorative justice, and forgiveness: An experimental psychophysiology analysis. *Journal of Experimental Social Psychology, 44*, 10–25.

Wood, A. M., Froh, J. J., & Geraghty, A. W. (2010). Gratitude and well-being: A review and theoretical integration. *Clinical Psychology Review, 30*(7), 890–905. doi:10.1016/j.cpr.2010.03.005

Wood, A. M., Joseph, S., Lloyd, J., & Atkins, S. (2009). Gratitude influences sleep through the mechanism of pre-sleep cognitions. *Journal of Psychosomatic Research, 66*(1), 43–48. doi:10.1016/j.jpsychores.2008.09.002

Wrosch, C., & Heckhausen, J. (2002). Perceived control of life regrets: Good for young and bad for old adults. *Psychology and Aging, 17*(2), 340–350. doi:10.1037/0882-7974.17.2.340

Wrzesniewski, A. (2003). Finding positive meaning in work. In K. S. Cameron, J. E. Dutton, & R. E. Quinn (Eds.), *Positive organizational scholarship: Foundations of a new discipline* (pp. 296–308). San Francisco: Berrett-Koehler Publishers.

Wrzesniewski, A. (2014). *Job crafting: Amy Wrzesniewski on creating meaning in your own work* [Video]. Retrieved from https://www.youtube.com/watch?v=C_igfnctYjA

Wrzesniewski, A., & Dutton, J. E. (2001). Crafting a job: Revisioning employees as active crafters of their work. *The Academy of Management Review, 26*(2), 179. doi:10.2307/259118

Wrzesniewski, A., McCauley, C., Rozin, P., & Schwartz, B. (1997). Jobs, careers, and callings: People's relations to their work. *Journal of Research in Personality, 31*(1), 21–33. doi:10.1006/jrpe.1997.2162

Zakrezewski, V. (2013, February 25). Teens who help, help their hearts. *Greater Good Magazine*. Retrieved April 4, 2018, from https://greatergood.berkeley.edu/article/item/teens_who_help_help_their_hearts

Index

Note: The letter *f* following a page number denotes a figure.

About the Author

 Chase Mielke is a writer, speaker, and award-winning high school teacher. He holds a master's degree in curriculum and instruction and runs www.affectiveliving.com, a blog dedicated to helping educators better understand and teach social-emotional learning. Mielke's work has been featured on CNN and on the websites *We Are Teachers*, *Edutopia*, *HuffPost*, and *Cult of Pedagogy*. He lives in Kalamazoo, Michigan, with his wife, Ashlee, and son, Maddox. Mielke can be contacted via AffectiveLiving.com/contact.

Related ASCD Resources: Professional Development

At the time of publication, the following resources were available (ASCD stock numbers in parentheses). For up-to-date information about ASCD resources, go to www.ascd.org. You can search the complete archives of *Educational Leadership* at www.ascd.org/el.

Print Products

The 12 Touchstones of Good Teaching: A Checklist for Staying Focused Every Day, by Bryan Goodwin and Elizabeth Ross Hubbell (#113009)

Fostering Resilient Learners: Strategies for Creating a Trauma-Sensitive Classroom, by Kristin Souers with Pete Hall (#116014)

Intentional and Targeted Teaching: A Framework for Teacher Growth and Leadership, by Douglas Fisher, Nancy Frey, and Stefani Arzonetti Hite (#116008)

Manage Your Time or Time Will Manage You: Strategies That Work from an Educator Who's Been There, by PJ Caposey (#119005)

The Resilient Teacher: How do I stay positive and effective when dealing with difficult people and policies? (ASCD Arias), by Allen N. Mendler (#SF114077)

Teach, Reflect, Learn: Building Your Capacity for Success in the Classroom, by Pete Hall and Alisa Simeral (#115040)

The Teacher 50: Critical Questions for Inspiring Classroom Excellence, by Baruti Kafele (#117009)

ASCD myTeachSource®

Download resources from a professional learning platform with hundreds of research-based best practices and tools for your classroom at http://myteachsource.ascd.org/.

For more information, send an e-mail to member@ascd.org; call 1-800-933-2723 or 703-578-9600; send a fax to 703-575-5400; or write to Information Services, ASCD, 1703 N. Beauregard St., Alexandria, VA 22311-1714 USA.

WHOLE CHILD
TENETS

1 HEALTHY
Each student enters school healthy and learns about and practices a healthy lifestyle.

2 SAFE
Each student learns in an environment that is physically and emotionally safe for students and adults.

3 ENGAGED
Each student is actively engaged in learning and is connected to the school and broader community.

4 SUPPORTED
Each student has access to personalized learning and is supported by qualified, caring adults.

5 CHALLENGED
Each student is challenged academically and prepared for success in college or further study and for employment and participation in a global environment.

THE WHOLE CHILD

The ASCD Whole Child approach is an effort to transition from a focus on narrowly defined academic achievement to one that promotes the long-term development and success of all children. Through this approach, ASCD supports educators, families, community members, and policymakers as they move from a vision about educating the whole child to sustainable, collaborative actions.

The Burnout Cure relates to the **safe** *tenet. For more about the ASCD Whole Child approach, visit* **www.ascd.org/wholechild.**